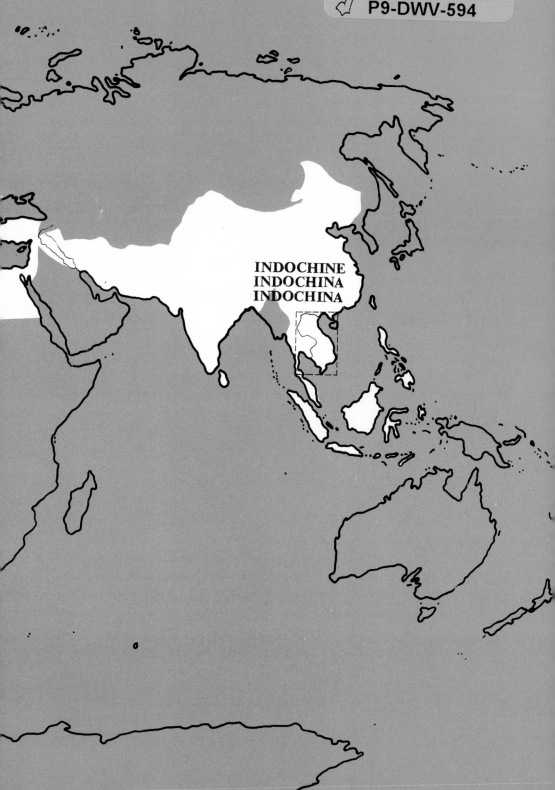

INDOCHINE
INDOCHINA
INDOCHINA

In the same series:

ARCHAEOLOGIA MVNDI

Series prepared under the direction of
Jean Marcadé, Professor of Archaeology
at the University of Bordeaux

BERNARD PHILIPPE GROSLIER

INDOCHINA

Translated from the French by James Hogarth

35 illustrations in colour; 110 illustrations in black and white

THE WORLD PUBLISHING COMPANY
CLEVELAND AND NEW YORK

CONTENTS

PREFACE

This series, which seeks to define the varying manifestations of archaeology in the different provinces of its vast domain, would not have been complete if it had not covered the Far East. This is not, in our western eyes, one of the classic fields of traditional archaeology; but the antiquity of the civilisations and the brilliance of the art that flourished there at so many different periods makes this area one of the most exciting and rewarding fields for future research. Faced with problems that are new or have for so long been neglected, compelled to create or adapt its methods to meet the specific conditions of investigation and interpretation, the science of archaeology may well achieve results in this area, both in the field of prehistory and of history, which will go far beyond its immediate objectives.

We can see this at once in the present volume. And yet – we must admit it, and Bernard Groslier makes the point clearly – the Indochinese peninsula has still been very little studied. The recent successes achieved in the excavation of prehistoric sites must not make us forget the vital tasks which still lie ahead: to carry out an accurate and exhaustive inventory of the contents of the various museums and collections, and to continue with exact recording, aerial survey work and the clearance of sites at present overgrown with scrub. And in addition to all this there is the critical re-examination of all the over-hasty theories and biased arguments that have been put forward in the past. Many of the celebrated wonders of Siam, Burma and particularly Cambodia have already become part of the universal heritage of art; but it is necessary to give them their proper place in the story of the civilisations of the past and of man's development since his earliest days. This is the task of Indochinese archaeology; and is this not the real aim of archaeology, to sustain and enrich our sense of man's achievement?

J. M.

THE BEGINNINGS OF INDOCHINA

I

The Background

Indochina is like a fan, its ribs formed by mountain chains, which is caught between the continents of India and China and spread out towards the Pacific. It descends from a height of over 10,000 feet to a submarine plateau so shallow that at a relatively recent geological period man could walk dryshod to Indonesia, towards which the Malay peninsula still extends its interminable length. Indochina belongs to the main land mass in the sense that its whole life flows from there, down the rivers which rise in eastern Tibet – the Red River, the Mekong, the Menam, the Salween, the Irrawaddy[1]. The rivers meander and spread their waters ever more widely as the mountains tail off, and finally deposit their alluvium for the benefit of man. But having taken its substance from the continent, Indochina turns its back on the land, pointing seaward with its deltas which are like gateways open to the ocean. It is a funnel through which Asia's superfluity of soil and of men can be filtered out and channelled towards the distant islands of Oceania.

The peninsula of Indochina extends from the Tropic of Cancer to the Equator. To this situation it owes its warm, oppressive climate, dominated by the south-western monsoon which brings all its rain in too short a period. The light soil which covers the harsh upland contours is all too easily eroded by mountain torrents; and the rich loam of the plains is gorged with water, constantly reshaped by the over-mighty rivers, and tormented by extremes of climate. The vegetation is luxuriant, so long as man does not interfere with it. Where he does – to the detriment of the soil – he succeeds in maintaining his own crops only as a result of a collective effort which enables him to even out the extremes of nature; but even then he has difficulty in coping with the oppressive climate and the endemic diseases which are rife in this country. Two natural species have, however, proved admirably adapted for man's support: rice, which cares little about soil so long as it is provided with an adequate water supply, and the buffalo, the only means of ploughing the mud in which rice flourishes. If to these we add the pig and the forest trees we have defined the simple biosphere from which man has been able to draw the means of subsistence[2].

We have still to note two contrasts. On the one hand there is the opposition, in the historical development of the area, between the mountains and the lowlands. It is not true to say that the mountains were uninhabitable and played no part in the history of Indochina. There were peoples living there – and some still living there – who achieved prosperity with less effort than the inhabitants of the lowlands, and who developed cultures of the greatest interest. But they are known only through oral tradition, so that their role in Indochinese history escapes us – though we may suspect their intervention on more than one occasion. The other distinction to be drawn is between the relative positions of India and China. The peninsula is physically controlled by the Chinese land mass to the north, and it was from China that the population of Indochina and part of its civilisation came. At first, however, there was a no-man's-land between Indochina and civilised China, which did not cross the Yangtse until a very late period. Usually the Chinese pushed in front of them other peoples whom they had not assimilated. These other peoples – the Burmese and Thai, for example – then found themselves in a world which was already within the Indian tradition, and came to terms with it. The influence of India, coming from the west, had more difficulty in making headway by the land route in a country whose lines of communication ran north and south; but it easily crossed the Bay of Bengal, which became indeed an inland sea for Indian trade. India was thus able to spread its civilisation widely in South-east Asia, as far afield as Borneo and even the Philippines[3].

Indochina thus forms a unity, though mainly perhaps as a result of the common history shared by its constituent parts. The separate parts have, however, been exposed to powerful influences profoundly different in their nature, their scale, and their effects. The great waves of human movement were from north to south – though their advance was not always due to sheer weight of numbers. From across the ocean which so rightly bears its name the influence of India – followed later by Islam, and then by Europe – has always been felt. To this day, and almost on the same parallel which used to mark the boundary between the two systems, the winds from the east still meet the winds from the west.

To complete this picture of the corner of human civilisation which we have chosen to study, it should be recorded that present-day Indochina – that is, Burma, Thailand, Malaya, Cambodia, Laos and the two Vietnams – contains a population of some 95 million distributed over more than three-quarters of a million square miles.

The appearance of Man

We shall not consider here[4] the origins of the population of Indochina, though human palaeontology draws the greater part of its evidence from archaeology. So far we have only some thirty skulls, mostly discovered in Tonkin and usually in Mesolithic and Middle Neolithic levels, which show the characteristics of each of the separate races at present known between China and Indonesia – and sometimes all of them at the same time. With this sample, restricted in space and time and insufficiently distinctive as it is, we can do no more than construct theories which to some extent may be no more than subconscious projections of accepted ideas about the present-day population[5]; and even the present population is by no means clearly defined. Moreover the various races are fitted into our time scale on the basis of evolutionary principles; and this is of course merely begging the question. In some cases the observed facts might be no less validly accounted for by isolation or regression, and this might well enable us to revise the presumed chronology. Our present hypotheses are of value only in so far as we seek to check them systematically against the facts as we find them on examining the material evidence and the records of the past. Unfortunately no one seems concerned to do this; and it must be admitted that the circumstances are not promising. Unfortunately, too, the prospects of future advance are poor; for the soil and climate of Indochina are peculiarly unfavourable to the preservation of unfossilised bony remains.

On the other hand we can sketch out – with increasing ease and indeed assurance as we approach more recent times – a picture of the industries of man as they have been discovered so far. They are identified with certainty in the Holocene; but the Palaeolithic material is still extremely inadequate, and we need in any case to define it geologically and stratigraphically rather than merely transpose as they stand the categories known in Europe. The oldest manifestations – Palaeolithic or, more cautiously, early Mesolithic? – are considered to be the industries of Anyathia (Burma), Kota Tampan (North Perak), Hoa-binh (Tonkin), and perhaps also Fing Noi (Siam). Then comes the Hoabinian and its characteristic implement, a stone shaped on one face so as to produce a chopper or crusher[6]. It is found on the Hoa-binh sites which provide the point of reference, in Laos, and above all in Malaya. It evolves very slowly, mainly by the selection of materials, into a Proto-Neolithic form – or at least a form which is considered such with the appearance of a crude basket pottery. In Laos it appears to have developed into an industry of flaked stone – unless this is an independent development to be compared with parallel data observed in the Philippines and to be referred to a common source.

It is also possible that the most recent levels of the Hoabinian reflect not a natural evolution but the influence of an independent Proto-Neolithic which is termed Bacsonian, after the sites which have been studied in the limestones of the province of Tonkin. The typical implement is a hand axe obtained by the flaking of a stone and the partial polishing of the cutting edge. The pottery improves and, most important of all, there appears (on a site in the plain of Da-but, Thanh-hoa) burial by inhumation with an elaborate ritual. This stage may be dated to the beginning of the 3rd millennium B.C.

The Neolithic, which later (after 2500 B.C.?) extended over the whole of Indochina, must once again be carefully defined; for it seems at least to co-exist with a knowledge of metal, which must have come from China, and the hitherto accepted theories on this point must now be reviewed in the light of the most recent discoveries. We shall confine ourselves to presenting very briefly the traditional views.

In general two main Neolithic systems are distinguished: one in inland Indochina, the other along the coasts. The former is characterised by an adze of lenticular section with a tanged heel, the latter by an adze of quadrangular section with no distinctive heel. The latter type also prevails in Indonesia, though the former is also found, without any known intermediary, in New Caledonia and on the northern coast of Australia. These observations have been explained by successive waves of migrant "Indonesians" from China. The matter is not, however, so straightforward as this. We must note, for one thing, the very considerable development of pottery, often turned on the wheel, and clearly influenced by China. With its stemmed vases and vase stands, this shows a real sense of structure, and the decoration – incised, stamped or glazed in large geometrical patterns – is superb. Finally there are the beautifully fashioned circlets of stone which have been found throughout the area; they are almost certainly of ritual significance, and inevitably remind us of the Chinese jade *p'i (Plates 1, 10)*.

The Neolithic adze apparently developed very rapidly into forms of perfectly rectangular section with a lug formed by two projections at an angle of 45 degrees, and hence known as shouldered adzes. It is more than likely that this shows the influence of similar implements in metal, the superiority of which was no doubt recognised by peoples which had neither the raw material nor the skill to work it. It should be noted that these shouldered forms are characteristic of the inland area, and are very rarely found in the coastal area or the islands. As time goes on, however, the presence of bronze is increasingly attested on all the "Neolithic" sites, by the discovery either of bronze objects – but these are rare because the soil does not readily preserve them – or of the double stone moulds used for casting them. Here again Chinese influence is manifest. The three sites which best illustrate the end of this development are Sa-huynh in Annam, Samrong Sen in Cambodia, and Gua Cha in Malaya.

Thus the chronological, or even typological, definition of a Bronze Age – or of a Metal Age – is not easy to establish. Right up to the beginnings of the first historical units we find material in stone, and in great abundance. Is this the result of the coexistence of backward upland cultures and of more advanced coastal cultures already in the Chinese or Indian orbit? We do not know: it is one of the many unsolved problems of the area.

However this may be, the use of metal – both bronze and iron – became dominant in the five or six centuries before our era. And here again we can define two large independent systems. Down the valley of the Mekong, scattered in pockets in Burma, in western Malaya, and as far afield as Sumatra we can recognise a megalithic civilisation, almost certainly associated with the identical and contemporary system in India. Sometimes the megaliths are simple standing stones; but the most notable monuments of this civilisation are the huge "jars" – cylindrical containers hollowed out of the local sandstone, sometimes reaching a height of 3 metres, which are mostly found in central Laos. At Ban Ang, the richest site, a cave was discovered which had apparently served as a place of cremation; and cremation was certainly an essential element in this culture. The jars and other monoliths no doubt marked the final place of burial of the ashes; as perhaps also did the "lids" found nearby – huge cir-

3   2

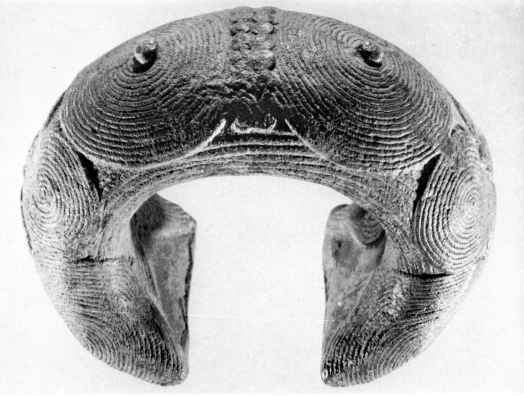

←1   4

15

18, 19, 20→

cular slabs with a rounded upper surface carved with crude figures of men and animals.

Almost simultaneously – as is shown by the characteristic bronzes which have been found associated with the jars – we find along the coastline of Indochina and as far away as Malaya, and beyond this on all the islands as far as Flores, a splendid bronze-using civilisation which is called the Dongsonian after Dong-son, the richest excavation site in the Thanh-hoa area. This was almost certainly a society of farmers, whose houses were built on stilts, who knew the buffalo, the pig and the dog, and probably grew rice as well; but they were also fishermen and seafarers who sailed magnificent canoes. They were excellent craftsmen in bronze, as is shown by the wealth of material discovered – socketed axes, hoes, shovels, knives, plates from armour, and so on *(Plates 2, 3, 4)*. At this period, too, there appear the famous bronze drums. Cast by the *cire perdue* process, they are shaped like mushrooms but with a flat top, and have on the sides handles in imitation of basketwork. They are richly decorated with pictures which are of immense value and interest. Similar drums – though on the whole less striking – are also found farther south, in Cambodia and on the Sunda Islands and Bali *(Plate 7)*. In these areas also have been found large vases, clearly destined for ritual use, in the shape of a flat gourd with decorated sides. There is a specimen in the Phnom Penh Museum which is one of the earliest and one of the finest of the plastic creations of Indochina *(Plates 5, 6)*.

We shall return later to the many problems posed by the origin and development of these civilisations. For the moment we need note only two points. With the help of many parallel features elsewhere and of the references in the Chinese writers we can date the flowering of the Dongsonian, at least in Tonkin, to the three centuries before our era. And we can deduce from the scenes represented in their art that the people of the Dongsonian culture believed in a life after death, and that their dead sailed away in "boats of life" to some paradise in the West, in the course of a ritual directed by priests comparable to the shamans of Asia – who also sail or fly about the world in their trances, communicating with spirits and learning from them about the future.

The Formation of the Historical Units

The appearance in Indochina of nations known to history is a result of the direct intervention of China and India and of their influence, which was predominant in the early period. Initially these influences can be apprehended only through the literatures of the two countries; later we have the inscriptions carved by the various peoples of the peninsula after they had adopted Chinese and Sanskrit as languages of civilisation and had taken over the scripts used by these languages to write their own languages. By archaeological means – that is, with the help of the material remains so far known and studied – we reach the same conclusions, though with much greater difficulty. The area of Chinese influence was directly colonised, and the material discovered is purely Chinese. Although, therefore, this material is thoroughly understood and exactly dated, it tells us nothing new and adds nothing to the information about the native societies of Indochina that we can glean from the official Chinese histories.

For the southern area we also possess a number of purely Indian and Western objects, certainly imported. But the chronology of the Indian styles of the first few centuries of our era is less exact than in China, mainly because of the lack of coins, but also because many monuments were built in timber or brick and have not survived. The literatures of India took little interest in the epic voyages of their seamen towards the East, and tell us practically nothing of the countries they discovered. On the other hand there has been a fair amount of archaeological research on this period in western Cochinchina, and to some extent also in Malaya and, more recently, in Thailand; and this has produced a rich harvest of finds which ought to throw light on the development of native arts under Indian influence. But so far these sites have failed to yield any inscription enabling us to fit them into the historical framework which can be deduced in essentials from the Chinese chroniclers. Thus, lacking any definite identifications and any firm stratigraphy or chronology, we cannot at present do better than date these objects broadly between the 2nd and 5th centuries of our era.

The Chinese Conquest

The Chinese, unified in 221 B.C. under Ch'in Shih-huang-ti, then began to extend south of the Yangtse into new territory which they knew already as an area from which they had long imported exotic products. To them it was known as the land of Yue, a country which – largely under the influence of the north and in reaction against these pressures – had achieved a political organisation of its own. It comprised the regions of Che-kiang, Fu-kien and Kwang-tung, and was allied with the chiefdoms of the Land of Lo – the delta of the Red River, no doubt inhabited by Proto-Vietnamese. Gradually all these princedoms, as far as Ha-tinh in Annam, were conquered by the Chinese and finally annexed under the earlier Han, to be organised in military districts each centred on a nucleus of soldier-settlers. The Annamite countries, at first grouped under the generic name of Nan Yue or South Yue and later known as Chiao Chi[7], remained Chinese territory until 907, in the T'ang period, in spite of the revolts led by the Trung sisters in A.D. 40 and by the three Li chiefs between 541 and 603. Throughout the area, therefore, Chinese influence was dominant, though no doubt the extent of its penetration varied in the different levels of society. The native hierarchy seems at first to have been respected, or at least used by the conquerors for their own purposes. In practice the infinitely superior Chinese civilisation gained complete control of the superstructure of society, with its system of ideographs, its literary traditions, and its administration based on the moral principles of Confucianism. Thus the Vietnamese perforce became part of the Chinese world; for even though the integration may well have been less effective at the level of the peasants, for example, the emergence of the Vietnamese as an organised society resulted from their incorporation into the Chinese scheme of things and from the development of the delta according to Chinese methods – the metal-shared plough, the use of human excreta as manure, intensive pig rearing, and above all the collective work on the building of dams and the regularly compartmented field system which provided protection against flooding. There followed the spread of the "market gardening" techniques which have always constituted the unshakeable strength of the Chinese, and which enabled the Vietnamese gradually to take into cultivation every scrap of low-lying land which appeared suitable, and eventually to extend their irresistible advance over the whole of southern Indochina. And finally it was because of China – or at least by the agency of the preachers who passed through Tonkin on their way to China – that Buddhism was established in these regions from the 5th century onwards. This was the only universal religion known to the Vietnamese world; and to it the Vietnamese owed the only art worthy of the name that they ever achieved.

The Land of Yue can be regarded, with reasonable certainty, as the area of the northern Dongsonian; but this has still to be demonstrated archaeologically, just as we have still to follow its dissolution and replacement by the pure Chinese culture. At Dong-son itself a terminal level has been found, with a fire, signs of pillage, and so on, which has been supposed to be a mark of the Chinese invasion. But in reality all that we see is the disappearance of the Dongsonian and the appearance – particularly from the beginning of the later Han dynasty – of Chinese material. This has been found throughout Tonkin, mainly in brick-built tombs. Apart perhaps from the pottery which, though of Chinese technique, nevertheless shows the influence of local traditions, the study of the material belongs to Chinese provincial archaeology and need not detain us here. Of native material, in particular of the civilisation of the original Vietnamese, we find nothing. We may hope, however, that excavation will one day solve some of the problems. The sites of the capital cities of the period are known: for example Co-loa (Phuc-yen), where air observation has revealed a system of earthworks (which *may*, however, go no farther back than the reoccupation of the town in the 10th century), Long-bien, the capital up to the middle of the 11th century, and Hanoi, which succeeded it. For the moment, however, there is an archaeological void to be filled.

The Influence of India

The Indian expansion into South-East Asia – for it was not limited to Indochina but extended also, with the same effects, into Indonesia – had causes and effects very similar to the expansion of China, though the means and the scale were different. Operating as it did mainly across the sea, it must have depended to a much greater extent on imitation and persuasion. This appears at any rate to have been so – though it is perfectly possible that there were colonising expeditions of a military character, as certain legendary traditions suggest.

Essentially it was to find new sources of supply of the exotic products – gold, precious stones, spices – which they then supplied to the Mediterranean world that the Indians sailed eastward. The pattern imposed by the monsoon, which made it necessary to spend at least one season on windward shores, and the need to build up economic cargoes of rare products from people who were ill-organised and not always easy to trade with, compelled the merchants to establish trading posts. Being Indians, they settled in communities, equipped with the whole religious, social and technical apparatus of their civilisation, which then radiated its influence into the surrounding populations. This was no new experience for a people who had already gradually Indianised the whole continent, as far as Cape Comorin, in the same way. Indian civilisation was then at its apogee under the Guptas, and ambitious men had every inducement – overflowing energy, perhaps a lack of space in India itself – to carve out new kingdoms for themselves in these rich and politically virgin lands. And in these areas the natives, apparently rapidly convinced of the superiority of the new civilisation, were easily won over to it, and consolidated their own rise with all the resources of the new order. Intermarriage and common interests led to the growth of an Indianised élite which was able in due time to fashion the great natural units of the peninsula into a number of separate kingdoms with splendid careers ahead of them.

This is, of course, no more than a reconstruction based on such inferences as we can draw from the facts known to us. It would be much more helpful to have even the scantiest historical records. But our conjectures are not entirely empty, for they are founded on at least two series of certainties: on the one hand the appearance of Indianised kingdoms which we can follow in the texts from the 2nd century onwards, and which must have been formed some time before this; on the other the Indian objects found by excavation.

The oldest of these "imports" are bronze figures of Buddha. Is this merely an accident of excavation, or is it rather the reflection of a historical reality, which seems to be confirmed by the considerable number of passages in the Buddhist scriptures referring to expeditions across the sea? In virtue of its missionary character Buddhism undoubtedly played a great part in the movement of Indian expansion, particularly as many sailors and merchants were ardent devotees. But it must also be noted – and it is a warning of how careful we must be in interpreting the facts – that the most important of the Indianised kingdoms of Indochina were Hindu, and more specifically Saivite. We cannot say more, however, than that eastern Indochina became basically Saivite while the western part became Buddhist.

Two phases are recognised in the effigies of Buddha. The first is the school of Amaravati (2nd and 3rd centuries), and its most notable piece is the Buddha from the river Kamara in Celebes. The second, which is more abundantly represented, consists of Gupta works of the 4th and 5th centuries: the most striking examples are the superb Buddha of Dong-duong, some small effigies discovered at P'ong Tuk in Siam *(Plate 9)*, and some very similar statuettes from the estuary of the Merbok, near Sungei Bujang in Malaya *(Plate 8)*. In some of these works the stylisation of the folds and the symmetrical treatment of the two forearms already point to a personal interpretation, and perhaps therefore to a local school.

The First Indianised States

If, however, we want to follow the formation of the first Indianised kingdoms, we must appeal to the Chinese historians, even though their data are not yet firmly related to the archaeological facts. With the conquest of Tonkin the Chinese came into contact with an Indonesian-speaking kingdom which they called Lin-i and we know as Champa. It is attested in A.D. 192 in the present-day district of Hué; and at this time began the struggle between "Sinicised" Indochinese and "Indianised" Indochinese[8] which was to end in the disappearance of Champa under the weight of Vietnamese numbers. By the 4th century inscriptions in Sanskrit and then in Cham, along with the Buddha of Dong-duong which has already been mentioned, show that Indian civilisation was establishing itself in this area. In the second half of the century a king named Bhadravarman, whose capital was probably Tra-kieu, founded in the mountain valley of Mi-son a temple dedicated to

Siva, of which no remains have been found. Nevertheless Rolf Stein's excellent work on the Chinese documents has made it possible not only to establish the precise course of events and to form some idea of the material civilisation of the early Chams, but also to define on the ground the territories of their cities. We must now await the archaeological investigation which has hitherto been lacking.

At the other end of the peninsula, which was in direct contact, Indian influence is much more evident. The Indians gave Lower Burma and the Malay peninsula the name of Suvarnabhumi, "the Land of Gold" – which indicates fairly clearly what they sought there. It seems reasonable to suppose that the deltas of the Irrawaddy and the Menam were occupied by Mon-speaking peoples, and the basin of the middle Irrawaddy by groups of the Pyu people, an outpost of the Burmese language group. The Pyus formed the important Indianised kingdom of Srikshetra, where the establishment of Buddhism is attested from the end of the 5th century by Pali Buddhist texts. Recent excavations at Hmawza have revealed remains which may date from the end of this period – in particular, stone urns containing the ashes of kings whose names are inscribed on the sides of the urns in Indian characters. But here again investigation has barely begun. The Mon country was known by the name of Dvaravati, and seems to have been centred on Thaton in Burma and Nak'on Pathom in Siam. It was also a centre of Buddhism which claimed to be the sole school of orthodoxy, and which eventually became dominant in South-East Asia. The earliest archaic Mon texts appear here in the 6th century, on architectural fragments in sandstone. The art of this country is known from a few remains of *stupas* (?) discovered, with the Buddhas already noted, at P'ong Tuk, and particularly from the fine "Wheels of the Law" from P'ra Pathom, fashioned from sandstone to commemorate the First Sermon of the Enlightened One *(Plate 11)*.

On the same site, though probably dating from a century later, were discovered the first Buddhist bas-reliefs on sandstone slabs, which no doubt

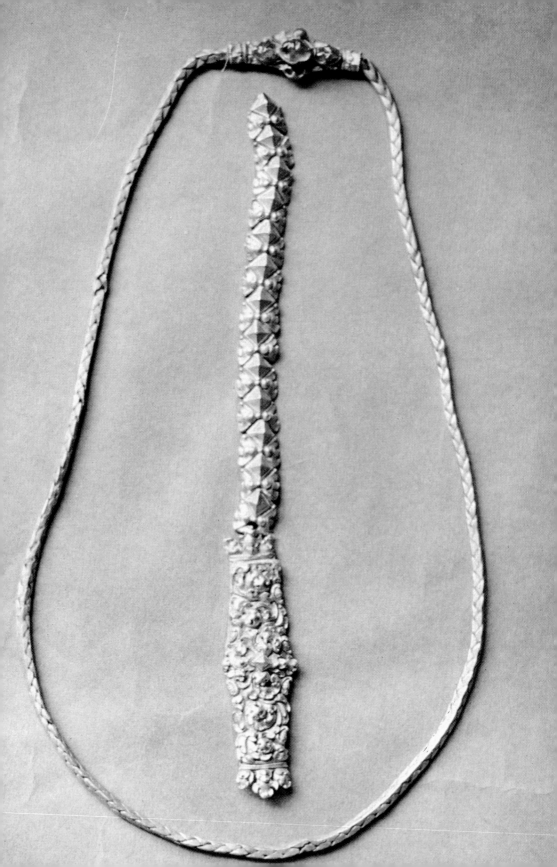

← 21, 22, 23, 24

decorated the bases of *stupas* built in brick. Nearby, at Wat P'ra Pathom and P'ra Men, Pierre Dupont excavated structures of this type, but they were altered at a later period and it is difficult to assign them with confidence to such an early date.

Farther south, in the areas of Ratburi and Ch'aiya, the Chinese writers record flourishing kingdoms which have not yet been identified by the archaeologists[8]. From this region, however, come the earliest sandstone statues found in Malaya *(Plates 12, 13, 14)*. They are Hindu, and more specifically Vaisnavite, in inspiration, and they show that by the end of the 7th century local schools had grown up and were already seeking to reach out beyond the traditional Indian techniques and create their own style of plastic art.

In the centre of this movement of Indian expansion, at the point where nature both imposed a halting place and offered space for the growth of a nation, on the western shores of the Gulf of Siam, there developed the most important of the indianised states. The only name we know it by is the one handed down by the Chinese writers, Fu-nan[10]. Mythological tradition claimed that it was founded by an Indian brahmin who married a local princess. The princess's father, king of the Naga, the Dragon Spirits of the Water – or perhaps, more prosaically, a chief who enjoyed their protection – gave this land to the young couple as a dowry, having first made it suitable for habitation by "drinking up the water which covered it". The allegory admirably illustrates the double process we have just summarised: on the one hand the arrival and establishment, by means of local alliances, of an Indianised élite, on the other the exploitation of the lands of the delta with the help of a drainage system, which could be carried through only by an organised society. For though the importance of the sea to Fu-nan, both for commercial and later for military purposes, is evident, and indeed was increased by the fact that its existence made communications between India and China easier and that the whole peninsula was developing, the working of the soil was an essential activity, and perhaps indeed became the main one when trade declined. And indeed observation from the air has revealed an impressive network of drainage channels between the Basak estuary and the Gulf of Siam, the skilful layout and extent of which suggest that this must have been a central feature of the economy. It is a monument unique in its kind which points to the sources of Funanese prosperity.

Once again, however, we must look to the Chinese historians for information about the early stages of Fu-nan's history. From the 2nd century of our era onwards they mention certain historical characters and speak of the Funanese conquests, which seem to have extended from eastern Cochinchina to Lower Burma, taking in on the way the Mon countries of Dvaravati and the upper Malay peninsula. The maharajas of Fu-nan sent ambassadors to China – which, having been temporarily cut off from central Asia, had to bring in imports by sea – and to the Murunda rulers of the Ganges valley. The end of the 4th century and the 5th must have seen a steady increase in trade with India, and consequently a strengthening of Indian influence. But it is certain also that the foundations of a native civilisation were being laid at the same time. One of the last great kings of Fu-nan was Jayavarman (*d. 514*), whose capital was in the uplands, on the present frontier of Cambodia between Ba Phnom and Angkor Borei. We see him as an adept of Siva – of whom the king was, as it were, the equivalent on earth – and more precisely of Siva Girisa, "dwelling on the mountain". The sacred mountain, the centre of the world and the dwelling place of the gods, was to become the fundamental symbol in the religions of the indianised states. Meanwhile, however, Buddhism was developing in parallel, for Funanese monks were later to be called to China to teach it.

The Funanese cities were founded in the drained area between the Basak and the sea. Ports and fortresses at the same time, their houses were built on stilts within great earth ramparts, criss-crossed by canals which served both for transport and for water control. Observation from the air has enabled large numbers of these sites to be identified, but only one has so far been explored, the site known by its present-day Vietnamese name of Oc-eo. This yielded a remarkable harvest of finds, which also made it possible to reclassify the many sporadic finds made in the area beyond the Basak. The finds include many imported pieces: Indian rings, seals, and jewels; coins of Antoninus Pius and Marcus Aurelius; Hellenistic intaglios (to be compared with a Ptolemaic lamp discovered at P'ong Tuk); Sassanid cabochons; Chinese bronzes of the later Han and the Wei dynasty. In short, there are all the signs of a considerable trade with the Mediterranean, particularly through the intermediary of the Indians. And given the absence of associated texts and of site identifications by correlation with the Chinese historians, these objects constitute our only dating points; though they are so miscellaneous and so impossible to date exactly that we can only assign them broadly to the period between the 2nd and the 5th centuries.

The lack of stratigraphy also prevents us from classifying any more accurately the objects of native production, though these are found in abundance. In particular we find evidence of an active industry devoted to the production of ornaments. The most interesting pieces are intaglios in hard stone often representing a royal personage, or scenes of ritual offerings; the finest are jewels in cast gold or tin, works of astonishing virtuosity. In these objects we have an important source of information on the material civilisation of the country.

Of Funanese architecture practically nothing has so far been studied. Probably it was mostly of timber. At Oc-eo, however, excavation has revealed what seems to be kind of small *cella* built in slabs of granite with mortise and tenon joints on brick foundations. A number of architectural elements in polychrome terracotta have also been discovered, copied exactly from Indian models and probably intended for the decoration of structures built in brick. The beginnings of sculpture are better known, at least towards the end of Funanese civilisation. Mention must be made in the first place of the astonishing Buddhas carved in wood and miraculously preserved in swamps *(Plates 15, 16, 17);* they are of Gupta inspiration and may perhaps therefore be dated to the 4th or 5th century. Then Pierre Dupont has very plausibly assigned to the reign of one of the last kings of Fu-nan, Rudra-varman (514–539[11]), the works discovered at Phnom Da, near Angkor Borei, the capital. They are Vaisnavite statues *(Plate 18)* and carvings in high relief on slabs of sandstone, designed to form an artificial cave – imitating, in an area where there no suitable rock faces, the rock sanctuaries of the end of the Gupta period. Although these works are evidently based on Indian models, the personality of the sculptor also comes through very clearly: already the Indianised states had assimilated their masters' teaching and were on the point of going beyond them. A striking example of this is the skill with which were they able to transform the monstrous shapes, half human, half animal, of their Indian models into figures of such perfect harmony and balance that they seem quite natural.

During the 6th century the immense movements of peoples impoverished what was left of the remains of the Roman empire and cut off its communications with the East by the traditional routes through the Middle East, until China under the T'ang dynasty, after its conquest of central Asia, became the only country to re-establish a link with Byzantium. Having thus lost their customers, the Indians likewise lost interest in their suppliers in the East; and in any case they were preoccupied with tremendous political upheavals, beginning with the invasions of the Hephthalite Huns. At the same time, perhaps, the indianised states may have felt strong enough to be self-sufficient – though their relations with India never entirely ceased and were maintained in particular by religious pilgrimages. From now on these states were to vie with one another in the development of their civilisations, now increasingly acquiring characters of their own, and also to come into conflict with one another. Among them Cambodia very rapidly stood out, and in the end was to dominate the whole of Indianised Indochina.

It was largely because they were the heirs of Fu-nan, and also because they occupied the most promising land, that the Khmer people achieved this predominance. They are found, speaking a language cognate to that of the Mons, in the middle valley of the Mekong, where by the 5th century they had organised themselves in a kingdom known as Chen-la[12], which may have grown at the expense of the Chams. Their national shrine contained a *linga* of Siva and was built on the hill of Vat Ph'u, but it is now covered by foundations of a much later period. We know nothing of their material civilisation, for none of the many sites identified has yet been excavated. Two of their kings, Bhavavarman (end of 6th century) and his brother Citrasena (attested in 615), finally subjugated Fu-nan and thus unified the whole of the middle and lower Mekong. In fact Fu-nan did not disappear immediately, and certain Malay princes later claimed to be its heirs – it may be with good grounds. But in practice its civilisation, and in particular its art, was taken over by the Khmers. We can trace this art throughout the 6th century, particularly in the form of a style of Buddhist statuary which continues the school of Phnom Da and proves that art is not necessarily associated with political success *(Plates 19, 24, 27)*. The architecture of the period is more difficult to study, for many buildings have not yet been properly described and there has been no excavation at all, although we know the sites of the main cities. Some of these sites, however, have yielded objects of great beauty, like the stuccos of Angkor Borei, which are an indication of what may remain to be discovered *(Plate 23)*.

The first great Khmer art is found in the reign of Isanavarman I (616–635), at Sambor Prei Kuk, the capital city built in the heart of the Empire. Some thirty buildings *(Plate 20)*, some of them the largest of their kind in Indo-china, are preserved here. The ritual planning, the architectural forms, even the decoration are still close to Indian models *(Plate 21)*. But the interpretation, the execution, and the relationships of the parts are Khmer, as are the statues treated fully in the round, which go far beyond the Indian carved stelae. The reigns of Isanavarman's immediate successors were peaceful if not glorious, and in one of them (Jayavarman I, 657–690) the peak of Khmer statuary was reached in the style of Prasat Andet. Architecture, on the other hand, seems to have been in decline – or at least to have frittered away its powers in building large numbers of brick towers of fairly modest size, with a simple floral decoration which soon degenerated. We can follow its general development even though precise information is lacking – for there has not yet been any excavation of sites of this period. This impoverishment becomes more marked after 717 and throughout the 8th century, during which the central government broke down to such an extent that the Chinese historians begin to speak of Tchen-la of the Land (the old Tchen-la proper) and Tchen-la of the Water, lying farther south (basically the old Fu-nan). Nevertheless, it was during this period that the Khmer civilisation was constituted and laid the foundations of its later supremacy.

Meanwhile Champa[13] was also growing in importance, though it was oriented towards the sea rather than the land. The Chams were shameless pirates who drew a considerable part of their wealth from incessant attacks on shipping along the great monsoon trade route. The 7th century was marked by fierce struggles with the Chinese, who had the better of it so long as their Empire remained united, and even succeeded in capturing the Cham capital, Tra-kieu, in 605. We know only from the texts the succession of monuments built at Mi-son in the reigns of Sambhuvarman (572–629) and Prakasadharma (653–686). To the latter's reign are attributed a number of pieces of sandstone sculpture – in particular a pediment and a pedestal – which form the style known as Mi-son E 1 *(Plates 61, 62)*. They show the dominant Indian style of the post-Gupta period, combined with an elegance of decoration and a feeling for the movement of human figures which were to remain characteristic of Cham art. These remains, along with a few Buddhist bronzes of the 8th century, enable us to detect a strong Cham influence on contemporary Khmer art, and perhaps also on the art of Malaya.

During the 8th century a new factor was to play a considerable part in the evolution of Indianised Indochina: the intervention of Indonesia. This country had achieved a remarkable upsurge, also under Indian influence. No less at home on the sea than the Chams, their linguistic brothers, and more powerful than they, first the kings of Srivijaya who held Sumatra, Malaya and the western part of Java, and then the Sailendra kings mainly based on Java – where they built Borobudur – dominated the southern seas and claimed with some appearance of reason to be the heirs to the dominion previously exercised by Fu-nan. They launched incessant raids on the Cham coasts, burning and looting, and also attacked Cambodia, where it seems likely that about the year 775 they destroyed the power of the Khmer king[14].

So long as we possess only scattered fragments of evidence and have no information derived from excavation in Indochina itself, we must fall back on the study of 8th century material in Malaya from an Indonesian point of view. It is true that the experts still hesitate to date within a century the fine bronze effigies of Lokesvara *(Plate 28)* discovered at Ch'aiya[15], or even the various pieces which have been excavated in Malaya *(Plate 26)*. Nevertheless they are evidence, direct or indirect, of the art of Indonesia. Nor must we neglect the Indian influence, which continued to make itself felt along these coasts. The influence of Pala art in particular can be recognised in the Buddhist effigies in the Taiping Museum *(Plate 30)*, which may thus date from the 9th century. And it is possible that these isolated pieces are to be associated with some sanctuaries recently excavated in North Perak which have yielded interesting stone reliquaries from the foundation deposit.

Indonesian influence is also found in Dvaravati, combined with the influence of the Khmers and, even more strongly, of India. The Hindu statues of Prachinburi, P'ech'aburi, Vieng Sra and Surat show strong Pala influences, and must therefore be assigned to the 8th century; they may perhaps account for some of the sculptured objects found in Cambodia which have already been mentioned. In Dvaravati as in Burma, however, Buddhism prevailed. After the Pyu dynasties, known by their funerary urns between the end of the 7th and the 8th century, we see the decline of this kingdom in the 9th. Although the main part of our information comes from the Chinese texts, some recent discoveries at Hmawza, near Prome, may perhaps yield some archaeological information about this period. They include the beginnings of Burmese architecture in the form of cylindrical *stupas* built in brick, strongly influenced by the art of Orissa, and in particular of the great Buddhist centre of Udayagiri.

29, 30, 31, 32, 33, 34, 35, 36, 37

39, 40, 41, 42 →

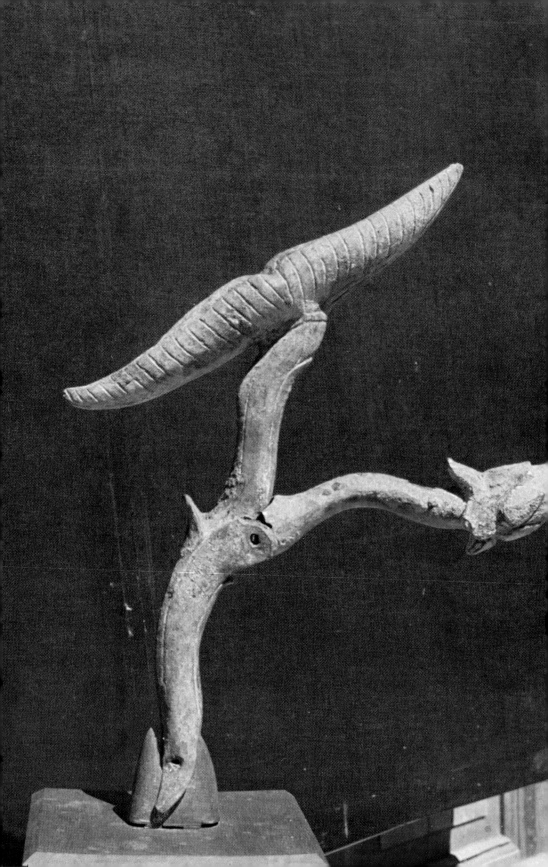

THE RISE OF INDOCHINA

The Dominance of Angkor

In the course of the 9th century the Khmer kings established themselves in the region of Angkor, near the Great Lakes, and laid the foundations of an empire which was to dominate the whole southern part of the peninsula for five centuries. Jayavarman II (802–850) freed himself from the Javanese overlordship and raised the *linga* of Siva, the symbol of his royal power, on the Kulen plateau as a visible representation of the Central Mountain. The art of his reign *(Plate 29)* was a renaissance which took something both from earlier traditions and from Cham models, but also contributed original features of its own, particularly in the field of statuary *(Plate 31)*. Indravarman (877–889) came down again into the plain between Kulen and the Lakes, where he was the first to lay out the network of irrigation channels which enabled the land to produce so abundantly. He inspired the powerful architectural style which reached its fullest expression in the Bakong *(Plates 33-35)*, the huge sandstone temple whose succession of terraces, each smaller than the last, rising to the final tower-sanctuary[16], represents the mountain which is the centre of the universe. Finally Yasovarman (889–900) carried out the tremendous hydraulic works which firmly attached the prosperity of Angkor to its soil, and crowned a natural mound in the heart of Angkor with the splendid temple of Bakheng *(Plate 36)*.

Archaeologically, this upsurge was marked by its use of the land; for the Angkor era was a veritable socio-economic revolution. Hitherto Cambodia had lived on rice – and lived well, judging from its rapid development. But it was a subsistence economy, merely taking advantage of the flooding of the rivers and the monsoon rains, with no engineering works of any importance. Gradually, no doubt, the Khmers became too numerous and too ambitious to be content any longer with this elementary solution, and sufficiently self-confident to attempt something better. In this field they were able to draw on Funanese drainage techniques and on experience acquired in the mountainous Tchen-la on the distribution of fresh water by gravity.

The choice of Angkor was no doubt determined by political considerations: it was the centre of the unified empire, which comprised the whole of present-day Cambodia, most of southern Laos, and the north-eastern part of Thailand. But it was also the only part of the country which could offer a large area of alluvial soil traversed by rivers which never dried up and near a lake which provided easy access to the sea and was stocked with inexhaustible supplies of fish.

Archaeologically speaking, Angkor is primarily an immense system of hydraulic works: main supply channels, dikes, reservoirs, field runnels, all designed to store up fresh water, collect rainwater, and redistribute it all to the meticulously planned network of rice-fields below. Thus the Khmers were able to compensate for the uncertainties of nature, to increase the yield of their land, and so to create an economic potential sufficient to support their expansion. This water supply network was continually extended so long as the empire continued to grow, until Angkor could show an uninterrupted succession of cities – that is, settlements provided with permanent irrigation – covering some 400 square miles. The pattern of these works was rigidly determined by the contours of the ground and the course of the rivers; yet the Khmers had the art of bending these technical requirements to their own purposes and achieving the most effective disposition of space round their monuments, so as to make them in reality what they were symbolically, the centre of the universe. It was this power that enabled them to erect an architectural complex which is, in the fullest sense of the word, unique. As a corollary, the enterprise, necessarily a collective one, required a rigidly centralised system and led inevitably to the dominance of an all-powerful king.

Nevertheless, the choice of Angkor was momentarily challenged. Jayavarman IV (921–941) – admittedly a usurper – moved his capital to Koh Ker in the north-east. But on his new site he maintained the well-tried techniques of the city – first the water supply system, then the temple-mountain which consecrated it *(Plate 32)*, in this case one of the boldest monuments ever created from stone. Rajendravarman (944–968) returned to Angkor, where he erected the superb Pre Rup, in which the plan of the temple-mountain is enriched with five terminal towers and associated buildings *(Plates 43-45, 120-123)*. Jayavarman V (968–1001) and Suryavarman I (1010–1050) carried this development a stage further. Their temples are more and more elaborate *(Plate 54)*, like the former's Phimeanakas with its continuous gallery round one of the upper terraces and the latter's unfinished Ta Keo with its colossal dimensions *(Plate 51)*. Meanwhile Khmer art could still produce delicately chiselled stone jewels like Banteay Srei (968) *(Plates 46, 47, 48)*, as well as countless local shrines. With Udayadityavarman II (1050–1066) the empire reached its peak. It now controlled, in addition to present-day Cambodia, the southern parts of Laos and Thailand, extending as far as northern Malaya. This power is made manifest in the enormous Baphuon, a temple-mountain with a profusion of roofs and galleries on each successive level which produces a rather confused effect, but with superb decoration and bas-reliefs; to say nothing of a rich flowering of shrines which decked every province of the empire with sumptuous ornament *(Plates 37, 50)*. Then – in spite of the political reverses which darkened the end of his reign – Suryavarman II (1113–1150) left in Angkor Vat the supreme and perfect image of Khmer art *(Plates 52, 55, 56, 57, 59, 124, 125, 127, 128)*. And yet this temple, one of the largest ever raised by the hands of man, is only one of a number of creations, any one of which – for example Beng Mealea or Banteay Samre[17] *(Plate 38)* – would be sufficient to immortalise the period which produced it. Already, however, there were ominous signs. Soon there were to be attacks by Cambodia's neighbours, who were not prepared to accept the rise of Angkor without a struggle. It is suspected also that there may have been internal troubles – perhaps a cleavage between a highly cultivated élite and the mass of the people who were worn out by war and overwhelmed by the demands made on then by their ruler's vast building works. Finally, the latest excavations show that the irrigation system, which had become the essential condition of life, was gradually becoming disorganised, mainly by silting up; and it was no longer being extended or even renewed, since all the country's resources were devoted to the temples through which the kings sought to ensure the continuance of their earthly glory into the life beyond. The looting and destruction of Angkor by the Chams in 1177 was a dramatic demonstration that the god-kings no longer held a special mandate from heaven.

One extraordinary man, however, was able to delay the inevitable end. Jayavarman VII (1181–1219) tried to save his people by his conversion to mystical Buddhism, given fantastic expression in dozens of temples larger than any that had hitherto been built, in particular the Bayon *(Plates 39, 53, 58, 118, 119. 130)*, which projects into space the image of the compassionate Buddha. Although this last spurt of energy was supported by glorious conquests and by the annexation of Champa, the end of Khmer power was in sight. It lingered on for two more centuries; but the empire was gradually torn apart, first by its old rivals and then, even more effectively, by the rising powers, the Thai[18] and the Vietnamese. Although the court had returned to Hinduism the ordinary people were gradually being won over to Theravada Buddhism, finding in it at last the peace they sought after carrying the burden of so much glory. The buildings of the period – which in any case were confined to Buddhist monasteries – were in wood and have for all practical purposes disappeared, apart from a few statues *(Places 60, 71, 131-134, 138-142)*; we have no evidence from excavation for this period. Since lapidary inscriptions also cease, the most recent centuries of Khmer history are also the least known.

Indianised Indochina and Angkor

The region of Champa developed vigorously until it was weakened by its fratricidal struggles with Cambodia, and Vietnam took advantage of the opportunity thus offered to it. Its buildings of the first half of the 9th century, in the Hoa-lai style, show us what the typical Cham sanctuary was like: a brick tower standing by itself, with parts of the door structure in sandstone. It is soberer than the Khmer equivalent, and more logical in that the volumes of masonry and the decoration still express the structure.

Indravarman II (875–898), a fervent Buddhist, founded a new kingdom at Indrapura (Quang-nam), and raised in Dong-duong, his capital, a huge building dedicated to Lokesvara *(Plate 64)*. The great sandstone altars have been found; they are decorated with sculpture which is both refined and brutal, and of great expressive force *(Plate 65)*. But in 982 the Vietnamese took Indrapura. The Chams fell back on Vijaya, in the Binh-dinh area; but here again they were defeated, and Vijaya was razed to the ground in 1068. King Harivarman IV (1074–1080) was able to halt this crumbling of the empire for a time, and even carried the war into the Khmers' own country, so that his successors were able to reign in peace until they were overcome in 1145 by the armies of Angkor.

Cham art reached its apogee during this period. At Khuong-my and particularly at Mi-son the style known as Mi-son A 1, which is found throughout the 10th century, is represented by some superb buildings, of powerful and delicate lines, which are the best examples of brick construction in Indochina *(Plates 41, 66, 67, 68, 69, 70)*. Javanese influence is manifest in the decoration, for example on the arcatures, but all the Cham vitality and freedom of movement is shown in the sculpture, the finest example of which is the pedestal of Tra-kieu *(Plate 63)*. Then, with the political decline, the architecture also becomes impoverished; the Po Nagar shrine at Nhatrang and Chan-lo, both of the end of the 11th century, show this trend.

It is true that Jaya Harivarman I (1147–1166) shook off the Khmers, and that Jaya Indravarman (1167–1190) was even able to surprise and burn Angkor; but soon Jayavarman VII of Cambodia avenged this raid and brought Champa into subjection until 1220. The constant pressure by the Khmers throughout the 12th and the first part of the 13th century is shown also in the influence of their art. The Binh-dinh style, to which all the works of this period belong, is one of deliberate imitation: it builds up a great series of false stories, each one slightly inset from the one below, so as to smooth off the angles and give the Cham tower the pointed silhouette of the towers of Angkor Vat *(Plate 42)*. We see this at Hung-thanh, which is later (beginning of 13th century), Thap-mam, and the Ivory Towers; then, at the end of the century, at Thua-tien, the Copper Towers and the Golden Towers. The decoration, particularly at Thap-mam, carries the stylisation of foliage to a point where it becomes a confused and inorganic tangle of finely drawn ornament. The carvings of the Silver Towers still retain a certain tranquil smiling grace, a reflection of the art of Angkor; but the fantastic figures of Thap-mam, which have been discovered literally by the ton, have no claim to merit other than their abundance and a certain wild grandeur.

The decline, however, continued inexorably. In 1225 the Vietnamese dynasty of the Tran successfully resumed the offensive. In 1283 the Mongols carried out raids on Champa. They were followed by the Vietnamese, who reached the Col des Nuages in 1366. The country was stoutly defended by King Che Bong Nga (1360–1390), who successfully resisted the Chinese, again temporarily in control of Tonkin, and even captured Hanoi; but in spite of his efforts the insatiable invaders from the north were able to conquer Vijaya in 1471, putting an end to the existence of Champa as a nation. Unlike Cambodia, however, and in spite of the sudden end that overtook them, the Chams – no doubt because they did not become converts to Buddhism – continued to the last to build brick temples dedicated to Siva, which allow us to follow the final developments of their architecture. Po Klaung Garai (end of 13th century?), Yang Prong, and Po Romé (which is probably to be dated to the beginning of the 16th century and is in any event the last Cham monument) mark this final phase. The architectural masses become progressively barer and more featureless, until finally they are no more than cubes plastered over with enormous excrescences piled one on top of the other, mere caricatures of the architectural devices formerly used to smooth off the angles. It is even more interesting to observe this decline in the field of statuary, which by a curious reversion returns to the theme of a figure carved on a stele and finally to a simple vertical slab decorated with the mere suggestion of a diadem and two eyes[19]. Thus, by a development which is almost unique, Cham art had gone through a complete cycle, first taking over a complete style from India and then arriving, twelve or thirteen centuries later, at forms which, if we had nothing else to go by, we should take for primitive idols developing towards anthropomorphism.

There is little to say, during the Angkor period, about the north of the Malay peninsula and the plain area of Thailand, since these areas were for all practical purposes Khmer colonies. It is certain, however, that the Buddhist art of Dvaravati continued to flourish. At Ku Bua, not far from Nak'on Pathom (where we know the buildings were used at least until the 10th century), there has just been discovered a very fine series of stucco reliefs, which must have served for the decoration of Buddhist monuments and are dated to the 9th and 10th centuries. But these countries were very quickly caught up in the empire of Angkor, to which in any case they belonged in language and culture. They were a valuable addition to the empire, for Suryavarman I, one of the greatest kings of Angkor, came from Ligor. Until the 12th century, therefore, the monuments found here belong to Khmer architecture. But in the light of the latest investigations two things are clear. On the one hand, even in Khmer buildings like those at P'imai and Lop'buri some details of the decoration suggest local craftmanship and indeed a local tradition *(Plate 37)*. On the other, Buddhist iconography was still active. Thus P'imai is dedicated to the Buddha, and a century and a half later Jayavarman VII added further shrines dedicated to the faith which he had embraced. Moreover in the art of his reign we find Buddhas which can be explained only by the survival of the Dvaravati tradition. It is in any case very probable that the form of Buddhism which was finally adopted in Cambodia came from the old Khmer colonies in Thailand, by way of Burma where it had also established itself.

The Rise of Buddhism in Indochina

It is a curious irony that India, which conceived Buddhism, should have rejected it utterly, and that this religion of renunciation should have found a fresh flowering in Ceylon and Burma under the most cheerfully warlike dynasties known to history. It was as a result of this transfer that Buddhism was able to win over a large part of the Hinduised are a and tomaintain itself there until the present day[20].

At the end of the 7th century the Burmese peoples founded in south-western China the kingdom of Nan-chao which in 832 subdued the Pyu people of Srikshetra; and these developments no doubt enabled the Burmese[21] of Arimaddana (Pagan) to begin their rise to power. They became civilised and were converted to Buddhism through contact with the Mon people; they did not, however, give up the worship of their ancestral spirits, the *Nats*, who after the final unification of the country under a king were symbolised by a pair of tutelary spirits dwelling on Mount Popa near Pagan. At first the Buddhism of the *Theras* was not the only form practised, and the Mahayana forms – in particular the sect of the Aris – also had their devotees. Meanwhile the rise of this new power in the north was paralleled by the growth of the kingdom of Pegu to the south, whose capital at Hamsavati is supposed to have been founded in 825. The rise of Pegu was due to its importance as an international trading centre – a role it still held in the 16th century, when it offered the Europeans a means of access.

46

←43, 44, 45

47, 48, 49→

The first great ruler of Pagan, the unifier of the country, was Anoratha (1044–1077), who became a convert to Buddhism, and conquered Thaton and its delta as well as part of Arakan. One of his embassies brought back from Ceylon a copy of the tooth which was a relic of the Buddha, and in honour of this he built the Shwezigon. It is important to note that, just as at Angkor, the power of the country depended on the establishment of a water supply system. The plain of Pagan, called in ancient texts Tattadesa, "the Dry Country", is afflicted with a climate of particular aridity: Anoratha therefore laid out a system of storage reservoirs and distribution channels, which his successors maintained and extended until finally they created Ledwin, "the Land of Rice". When the archaeological investigation of this area, by aerial and stratigraphical study, has been completed, as it has been in Cambodia, we shall understand one of the determining factors of Burmese history[22].

Under Kyanzittha (1084–1112) the kingdom developed still further. A great admirer of the Mon civilisation and of Buddhism, he brought artists from Thaton and repaired the temple of Bodh Gaya, near Benares; and by opening up his country to these two influences he raised its art to a peak which marks the apogee of Pagan. Alaungsithu (1112–1165) was also a builder, but his immediate successors were too busily occupied in fighting for the throne to have time for such activities. In 1190 Buddhism, which had been reformed in Ceylon under the great King Parakramabahu, was introduced by the Mon monk Chapata; it won the day, though not without a struggle, and finally spread throughout the Indianised peninsula. Up to the end of the 13th century the last kings of Pagan continued to erect considerable monuments which give no indication that the end of their power was near.

At the origin of the Burmese school of art which grew up at Pagan[23] we must undoubtedly place the Mon *stupas*, with their characteristic ogival shape. The oldest are thought to be those of Bébé Paya, Payama and

Payagyi Pro tome. On the same site the shrine of Zegu shows the technique of the vautain voussoirs of brick, which the Pyus had already completely mastered. The source of this technique is uncertain: it is tempting to derive it from China, at least as early as the former Han, but the system may also have been employed in India, whose influence on the architecture is quite evident. We have little knowledge of the later development of this Pyu art, after the destruction of the kingdom of Prome at the end of the 8th century. We know only that the decoration of Buddhist shrines with terracotta plaques was already in favour. We must probably assign to the 10th century the laterite base of the *stupa* of Zokhetok near Thaton and some reliefs from this area, also on laterite. At Pagan the oldest buildings belong to the 10th century; in particular one of the town gates, the Sarabha, and the *stupa* of Bupaya, which is based on Mon models but tends towards a bell-shaped silhouette. The *stupa* of Ngakyawenadaung (perhaps showing Tibetan inspiration) and the temple of Nat Hlaung-Kyaung, the only Brahman shrine on the site, are attributed to King Taungthugyi (about 915–931). To the end of this century – already reflecting Sinhalese influence– probably belong the two Peitleik temples, *stupas* surrounded by galleries decorated internally with terracotta reliefs illustrating the earlier lives of the Buddha, the *jatakas (Plate 72)*.

It was Anoratha who undertook the erection of the chain of temples which finally covered the plain of Pagan and rivalled the stone forest of Angkor. He is said to have brought Mon workmen from Thaton; certainly he built *stupas* inspired by Mon art, in particular the Shwesando (1057) *(Plate 75)* and the Lokananda (1058). The imitation of Indian models is recognisable also in the *stupa* of Seinnyet Nyima *(Plate 85)*. In Burma, however, the *stupas* are usually raised on a base of several tiers, decorated with reliefs. The masterpiece of the type is the Shwezigon (completed in the reign of Kyan-zittha), which inspired many other *stupas* at Pagan, like the Dhammayanzika of King Narapatisithu (1196) and the Mangalacetiya (1274). At the same time another type of shrine more characteristic of Burmese art begins to take shape. It consists of a central block surrounded by a gallery, on top of which, pointing towards heaven, is a *stupa* or tower symbolising the Central Mountain of the Universe. The narrow spaces contained in the interior were the equivalent of the caves hollowed in the sides of a mountain in which ascetics were accustomed to meditate. The first of this type was probably the Kyaukku Umin, which may go back as far as the 10th century and was completed by Narapatisithu.

More interesting is the Pithakathaik *(Plate 80)*, founded in 1058 and restored in the 18th century, which imitates the native style of building in wood, with its series of roofs of decreasing size, each one on top of the one before. The same tradition is found in the Mimalaung Gyaung of 1174, and this is probably the explanation of many unusual features of the structure[24].

Finally, in considering the elements from which this art was built up, we must note the part played by King Manuha, who was taken prisoner at Thaton and brought to Pagan. He erected the Nan Paya *(Plate 77)*, a huge hall built on brick pillars clad with stone, crowned by a tower inspired by the Indian *sikhara*. To him also[25] we owe the temple which bears his name, with the colossal statues of Buddha in the interior: a pattern which was extremely popular in Burma and Siam. Kyanzittha repaired the Bodh Gaya, and was inspired by the accounts given to him of the shrines of Udayagiri by Indian monks from Orissa to construct the Ananda temple (about 1105) *(Plates 73, 74, 79, 92)*. It is square in plan, a huge central pillar supporting a *stupa* in mid-air, surrounded by two concentric corridors lit by windows approached by narrow passages, and with four porches in front of the entrances. Kyanzittha was also responsible for the Nagayon, while his wife built the Abeyadana: both temples of Indian type surmounted by a *sikhara*, but also strongly influenced by the native architecture in wood. These were models for the Shwegugyi (1131). In 1144 Alaungsithu achieved in the Thatbyinnyu *(Plate 81)* a still more elaborate structure, in which the central building was raised on an enormous base and contained a very large seated

Buddha. The culmination of this trend was the Dhammayangyi built by Narathu (1167–1170) and its later imitations, the temple of Sulamani at Minnanthu (1183) *(Plate 90)* and the temple of King Htilominlo (1218) *(Plates 89, 91)*.

The most interesting aspect of Burmese art is its decorative techniques. We have already mentioned the terracotta reliefs. In the Ananda they are glazed; the same thing is found in the Mangalacetiya (1274) *(Plates 73, 74, 94)*, and the Dhammarajiha (1196) is decorated with reliefs in painted stucco. Finally the frescoes of Pagan would merit detailed discussion, for they are almost unique in Indochina. They are found as early as the Nandamannya *(Plate 93)*, where the Mahayana and Hinayana themes are combined, as in the later Payathonzu. They would require to be studied along with the influence of salvationist Buddhism in Bengal, which also inspired Jayavarman VII at Angkor. Nevertheless the themes of orthodox Buddhism prevailed in the end, as in the Patothamya (end of 11th century?), the Kubyaukgyi (1112) *(Plate 84)*, the Lokahteikpan (1113) dedicated to the life of the Buddha, the Kondawgyi (13th century) which is decorated with *jatakas*, and the cave temples of Kyanzittha *(Plate 84)* at Nyaung-U (12th century?), which were strongly influenced by the Chinese painters.

THE GROWTH OF NEW POWERS

III

Independent Vietnam

Although until the 13th century the Indianised states offer the greatest interest to the archaeologist by reason of the abundance and quality of their
material, they were not the only states which developed in Indochina. Vietnam, although in many respects no more than a province of Chinese civilisation, achieved its independence and started the move southward whose consequences for Champa we have already seen. It was given its opportunity by
the fall of the T'ang dynasty: from 939 onwards Tonkin recovered its autonomy under the name of Nam Viet, and its various feudal lords split up the
territory into a number of separate geographical units. It was not until 968
that the country was unified by the Dinh dynasty; then in 979 it passed into
the hands of the Le, who conquered north Champa. In 1010 the Ly dynasty
established their capital at Dai-la-thanh near Hanoi. Many finds have been
made there, revealing a well developed art in terracotta: decorated tiles,
architectural elements, and so on, which are admittedly of Chinese inspiration but nevertheless show a lively imagination. During the same period pottery kilns which were probably established by Chinese craftsmen produced
a type of pottery improperly called Thanh-hoa, from the province where it
has been found in greatest quantity *(Plates 83, 86, 87, 88)*. It belongs to the
Sung tradition; but with its robust shapes, its nervous decoration with
streaks of brown on a light background, it produced some splendid pieces
which are among the finest creations of the period.

A Buddhist art of some consequence also developed. Near Thien-khe
(Tuyen-kang) have been found caves decorated with frescoes which are
thought to date from the 10th century. At the pagoda of Phat-tich (Bac-
ninh) some interesting sandstone reliefs have been excavated, belonging to
the first foundation on the site by the Chinese general Kao P'ien, which is
dated between 866 and 870. They show a Chinese technique, but also reveal
strong Indian and perhaps central Asian influences which prove that Tonkinese Buddhism was still in contact with its sources. A second *stupa* was

erected here in the reign of King Ly Thanh-tong (1054–1072), the conqueror of Vijaya. It was the first of a series which are grouped together as the Ly style. Among these must be mentioned the *stupa* of Long-doi-son (Ha-nam), built by Ly Nhan-tong (1069–1128), which had to stand up to attacks by the Khmers. The tower of Binh-son (Vinh-yen) is thought to mark the end of this style, towards the middle of the 12th century, along with the altar of the pagoda of Thien-phuc (Son-tay) of 1132, in which some signs of Cham influence can still be seen. This was the last example of a distinctively Vietnamese style. Even these few remains, however, are sufficient to show us that Tonkin may not have been entirely closed to the various currents which created Indochina.

The Thai Infiltration

Meanwhile in the heart of Indochina, like the Burmese and the Vietnamese before them, the Thai were on the move, filtering down through the valleys towards the south. They were organised in feudal princedoms, and their leaders were also the propitiators of the spirits of the soil. Although they had long lived within the Chinese orbit, occupying the uplands while the Sons of Han were colonising the coastal plains and the rich valleys, they were not Sinicised like the Vietnamese[26]. Thus, gradually moving south to escape the Chinese, they were foot-loose, and Indian territory was all the more attractive to them as it offered the opportunity of establishing a stable political unit.

At first the Thai chiefs were content to establish themselves in the uplands, above the great empires of the plain. In the south-west of China they formed part of the Tibeto-Burmese federation of Nan-chao[27] in the 11th century. They advanced to the south-east but were unable to make headway against the numbers and the stubborn resistance of the Tonkinese, and could do no more than occupy the lands of Muong-then and Lai-chau. To the south-west they were for long held in check by the kings of Pagan. In the end they found the line of least resistance between these two powerful neighbours, in the form of Thailand as we know it today, a country built up at the expense of the Mons – who never succeeded in establishing a strong political unit – at the line of junction between the Khmer and Burmese empires.

The Crisis of the 13th Century

The redrawing of the map of Indochina was largely brought about by a series of local crises and foreign intrusions which took place during the last two-thirds of the 13th century, eliminating the moribund structures of the past and offering scope for the rising ambitions of new men.

In Cambodia, as we have seen, the decline began – or at any rate became more marked – after the death of Jayavarman VII. It could not be halted, for the whole economic organisation was falling to pieces: the growing weakness of authority, political reverses, the wasting away of material resources, the ousting of belief in the god-king by Buddhism – each of these things must have increased the impact of the others and in turn been affected by them[28]. Taking advantage of the decline of Angkor, the Mon colonies of Lop'buri *(Plate 98)* became practically independent in the middle of the 13th century; the kingdoms in the north of the peninsula were already independent by the beginning of the century. The Mon kingdom of Haripunjaya, which had always enjoyed autonomy, grew in authority. At the beginning of the 12th century – already commemorating a victory over the Khmers – King Aditaraja erected in his capital at Lamp'un Vat Kukut, which was restored in 1218. It is a solid building in brick, with five cube-shaped stories of decreasing size, decorated on each face with three large Buddhas in stucco under an arcature. It is in effect a development of the commemorative monuments which we have already noticed in Dvaravati. The same pattern is found, with the addition of strong influences from Angkor, in Vat Mahathat at Lamp'un, which in its present state dates from 1447, and – more interesting still – in the Sat Maha Prasada at Polonnaruwa in Ceylon, which was probably built by Mon pilgrims[29].

Then, at the very moment when the ancient kingdoms were beginning to disintegrate, the Mongol conquest, which not only mastered China but launched its furious cavalry charges throughout the whole of the Far East, turned its full force against these societies which were already undermined. It is true that in Vietnam repeated assaults by the armies of Kublai were beaten back between 1257 and 1281, and that in Champa a Mongol attack by sea was repulsed in 1284 and a Mongol force which had passed through Tonkin was wiped out in 1285. But in Burma Pagan was overrun in 1287, and henceforth China was always pressing at the passes of eastern Tibet.

A number of Thai chiefs, already established on good bases, were not slow to take advantage of the chances offered by these mighty hammer blows. Mangray conquered Haripunjaya and in 1296 founded the kingdom of Chiengmai. Rama Kamheng carved out a kingdom which stretched from Vientiane and Luang Pra'Bang to Ligor and Pegu, and in 1287 established his capital in the centre of it, at Sukhot'ai. The Shan chiefs established their control over the successors of the kings of Pagan, while the Thai chief Wareru ruled over the Mon delta; and the Burmese kings had to take refuge in the princedom of Taungu. Finally, as we have seen, Champa was gradually being eaten away, leaving only Cambodia among the ancient Indianised states, reduced to a mere shadow of its former splendour.

After the 13th century the monuments of Indochina are of less and less significance. This is partly because there have been no excavations or systematic studies in this field; but also because the few items of interest that have been found show the use of earlier themes by cultures which themselves are not original and which – whatever their historical interest – never achieved any distinction of their own.

The Thai Kingdoms

For the main elements in their civilisation the Thai depended on the Mons, who still made up the mass of the population in the ricefields of the plain. From them they took the Buddhism of the *Theras*, and with it many influences from Burma, where this religion had just become dominant. Simultaneously – first in the former Khmer colonies in eastern Siam, then at Angkor itself, which they finally destroyed in 1431 after attacking and looting it for for the last hundred years – they took over from the Khmers the whole apparatus of the state, together with the last glimmers of their splendid art.

Thai art proper was formed between 1230 and 1318, in Rama Kamheng's twin capitals of Sukhot'ai *(Plates 97, 99, 100, 101)* and Sawank'alok *(Plates 95, 96)*. The characteristic monument of this architecture of stucco-covered brick is a tower derived from the Khmer shrine, usually with a large timber-roofed hall in front of it designed for gatherings of monks and containing a statue of the Buddha, often of colossal size. The monastery was completed by bell-shaped *stupas* of increasingly tall and slender lines, and sometimes also by a reliquary shrine raised on a base of many tiers: Wat Mahathat at Sawank'alok *(Plate 95)* is the best specimen of the former type, Wat Mahathat at Sukhot'ai *(Plates 99, 101)* and Wat Chedi Chet Theo at Sawank'alok the most interesting examples of the latter. In statuary – mainly Buddhas in bronze – Sukhot'ai created a genuine style of its own, based on the art of the Bayon, perhaps on Chinese models, and above all on a firm will to give expression to the new faith. The great Buddha in Wat Mahathat at P'itsanulok is one of the finest achievements of this style, with its modelling of rounded masses meeting at sharp angles; but unfortunately the style had become stereotyped by the end of the 14th century and throughout the following century produced nothing but tedious repetitions. These attempts, at least in the early days, were not the only ones. At Chiengmai, which carried on the heritage of Haripunjaya while at the same time seeking inspiration from Ceylon, there was a school in the reign of U T'ong which began by continuing the styles of the Mon art of Dvaravati, and then came under the influence of Sukhot'ai[30].

In 1347 Ayuthya became the capital of a unified kingdom. As a result of the constant flow of the spoils of war from Angkor, and of their ambition to take the place of Angkor, the Thai kings deliberately moulded their art into a mere copy of the art of Angkor, which fascinated them. This influence was predominant from the 15th to the 17th century. The tower-sanctuary lost all organic logic when it was reproduced in brick: the mouldings and projections, multiplied indiscriminately, altered its silhouette and deprived it of any meaning. Nevertheless it was often combined with the *stupa* or the reliquary shrine to produce hybrid forms which had a certain elegance of their own – sometimes deceptively concealing the poor craftsmanship of their builders. The main temples at Ayuthya, from Wat P'ra Ram (1369) to Wat Sri Sanp'et (1492) *(Plate 103)*, show this process at work. The statues of Buddha, seeking to reconcile the school of U T'ong with the school of Sukhot'ai, and influenced also by Khmer works, are too overloaded with ornament and, above all, were produced in too great quantity to have any life of their own.

In the south, round Ch'aiya, the same characteristics are found in accentuated form in the school of Grahi, which had carried on the tradition of Khmer plastic art. In the north, on the other hand, and particularly in the reign of the pious King Tiloka, who in 1455 built a replica of the temple of Bodh Gaya, the model was provided by the Pala-Sena art of India, giving rise to works which were undoubtedly orthodox but cold and impersonal.

The monasteries were decorated with paintings of the greatest interest, but we know little of the development of this tradition. The frescoes in the cave of Silpa at Yala, which unfortunately are badly damaged, are perhaps to be dated to the 10th century. Wat Si Ch'um at Sukhot'ai (1286) *(Plate 100)* contains some carved slabs of great beauty representing scenes from the life of Buddha, which show that at this period Thai draughtsmanship had achieved complete technical competence.

It is with the paintings decorating the royal burial chambers of Wat Rat Burana (1427) at Ayuthya[31] that we begin to be able to study this technique. They show both a strong Chinese influence and an original style of genuine narrative power. The frescoes of Wat Mahathat at Ratburi (end of 15th century), Wat Yai Suwannaram at Petburi (beginning of 17th century) and Wat Budhaisawan at Ayuthya (end of 17th century) enable us to follow the development of this style, which can achieve fine effects by a skilfully distributed composition of tones in flat colours and a sense of aerial perspective.

Finally we must mention the establishment of pottery kilns at Savank'alok and Sukhot'ai by workmen from China in the 13th century. In seeking to imitate the celadons and later the blue-and-white style, the craftsmen of Siam produced original work, with robust shapes and a satiny glaze, which were so popular that they were exported to all parts of Indochina and as far afield as Indonesia[32].

It was at Bangkok that the capital of Siam was established in 1767, dominating not only the present country of Thailand but also the west of Cambodia and the whole of Laos along the Mekong. Nevertheless, despite the splendour of the pagodas and palaces of the new city, the art was mechanical and repetitive. The execution, however, is still remarkable, particularly in works of genuinely native inspiration like architecture in wood or decorative painting *(Plates 108, 108, 110)*. And this, it must be noted, is the only living form of art in indianised Indochina at this period.

One other province of Siamese art still remains to be mentioned, the Laotian school. The first kingdom of the Lao Thai, that of Lan Xang, had been founded by Fa Gnum (1353–1373), together with the two capitals between which the country was divided, Luang P'ra Bang and Vientiane. The latter was situated in former Khmer territory, and the local Buddhist art therefore began with poor copies of the statuary of the Bayon. In the north there were a number of armed incursions by the Burmese; hence the pagodas in the Burmese style at Muong Sin and Luang P'ra Bang itself. But in essence Laos was dominated by Siam, and consequently it was the art of Ayuthya that provided the model. Nevertheless, an original culture developed in these enclosed inland areas, reaching its full power in the Th'at Luang at Vientiane (*Plate 105*), founded by King Setthath'irat in 1586. The central *stupa*, slender and powerful at the same time, decorated with sober mouldings and surrounded by a timber cloister, is one of the great achievements of Buddhist architecture. There are also some Laotian Buddhas of this period which are of outstanding quality with their delicate and graceful lines. We can therefore see indications of a real artistic individuality which had neither the occasion nor the means nor the geographical scope which might have enabled it to produce works of greater impact.

The Survivors

Even when they were forced by the constant harrying of the Thai to leave Angkor and transfer their capital to the area of Phnom Penh, in the centre of present-day Cambodia – where in the 18th century they again found themselves threatened by the Vietnamese who had arrived in Cochinchina – the Cambodians, though they no longer dominated southern Indochina politically and aesthetically, still continued to build monasteries and to decorate them *(Plate 111)*. But not a single building has survived from a period earlier than the beginning of the 19th century; nor has there been any excavation of their capitals of the 16th and 17th centuries, the sites of which are known. A few statues in wood, ranging in date between the end of the 16th century and the present day *(Plates 131, 132, 133, 134)*, are the only landmarks in the development of their art, along with a few reliefs carved at Angkor in 1550 on 12th century panels which had remained unfinished[33]. They are enough to suggest that the plastic genius of the Khmers had not been extinguished, even though it was no longer in the service of a commanding power, and to show that the Thai who dominated the country were content to carry on the artistic traditions they found there[34].

Burma, on the other hand, did not suffer a political decline: it was constantly at odds with Siam and was almost always victorious in the fierce wars between the two countries. Indeed, by one of the curious chances of history, the Mons achieved a resurgence which for a time threatened the Burmese predominance; and the kingdom of Pegu, under a Thai dynasty, remained firmly established until the middle of the 16th century. In the centre of the country the power of Taunggu became dominant after 1347, and even succeeded in reunifying the whole country under Tabinshwehti (1531–1551) and his son Bayinnaung (1551–1581), who twice captured Ayuthya. In the north the kingdom of Ava, founded in 1364, and the Thai chiefdoms survived, thanks to the struggles between the larger states and to the periodic slackening of central control. Finally the dynasty of Ava became dominant under King Anaukpetlun (1605–1628), but then fell apart under Chinese, Manipuri and Thai attacks. Alaungpaya (1752–1760) again restored unity, and his dynasty lasted until the British conquest. Its main centre was Mandalay, where Bodawpaya (1782–1819) had established his capital. It is interesting to see this king repairing and extending the old irrigation network at Mandalay, on a pattern which has been revealed by archaeology – a pattern which did not change throughout the centuries, for it was the only means of maintaining life. These rulers, too, erected a great number of Buddhist monuments, often of colossal size. But here, too, it seems as if some spring was broken, for the huge scale of these buildings cannot conceal their barren formalism. We need, therefore, mention only the famous *stupa* of the Shwe Dagon at Rangoon, founded in 1372 and enlarged in 1460 by the Mon queen Shinsawbu, which in its final form attained a

Paintings on lacquered screen. Collection of Prince Piya Rangsit, Bangkok. Bangkok style; 19th century. Scenes of court life, from Thai tales. (phot. B.P. Groslier).

height of 105 metres and a diameter of 450 metres. In 1790 King Bodawpaya began to build at Mingun the temple of Pondaw, which is 150 metres long at the base and according to the original plan was to be over 100 metres high. It was abandoned when it had reached 65 metres, but even as it stands it is probably the largest mass of brick in the world, estimated to contain more than a hundred million bricks.

It was only in the field of painting – which had received fresh stimulus from the influence of Chinese calligraphy – that Burmese art continued to produce fresh and original work, of which unfortunately there has not yet been any systematic study *(Plates 82, 92, 93)*.

The Dominance of Vietnam

The Ming dynasty managed to re-establish Chinese overlordship in Tonkin in 1413; but the Vietnamese, having escaped the Mongol threat, were in no mood to put up with this control for long. They were able to free themselves under Le Loi (1428–1433), and the dynasty of the later Le reigned until 1527. It completed the conquest of Champa and reorganised the country into a veritable empire. The 17th century was marked by interminable struggles between the feudal clans of the Trin and the Nguyen, but these did not prevent groups of Vietnamese from penetrating into Cochinchina and settling along the Mekong, and even encroaching on eastern Cambodia. The Nguyen proclaimed themselves emperors, but in 1773 their authority in the north was shaken by the revolt of the brothers of Tay-son. Finally Gia Long (1802–1819) defeated them and unified the country.

Although it did not succeed politically this brief intrusion by China does seem to have stimulated a new wave of Chinese influence in Vietnam, at least among its ruling classes – as if the emperors who were seeking to unify the country could find no better source of inspiration or more perfect model than the Chinese system. The result was, unfortunately, to sterilise any local aesthetic sensibilities. Apart from the sturdy fortress of the Ho (Thanh-hoa), built in 1397, hardly a trace of any creative force can be found in Vietnam from this period. The only things worth mentioning are the royal tombs at Lam-son (Thanh-hoa), ranging in date from 1428 to 1500, which have yielded some fine funerary stelae, and the stone bases of the palaces, decorated with Chinese dragons and phoenixes.

The pagodas and tombs of the 17th century are mere copies of earlier work. Particularly in Tonkin, however, there was an architecture in wood of great virtuosity and often of great beauty. Examples of this are the pagoda of Ninh-phuc (Bac-ninh) and above all the *dinh*, communal dwellings which continued into modern times an ancient type of house built on stilts[35]. Finally at Hué, the capital of the unified empire, the Nguyen emperors built a fortified palace *(Plates 107, 113, 114)* and tombs *(Plate 112)* which reflected the ideals they took from China – in the orientation determined by the geomancers, the relationship of the different buildings, the layout of the tombs, and the great array of esplanades and terraces at Nam-giao where each year was celebrated the harmonious union of Earth and Heaven in the person of the Son of Heaven, the centre of the Middle Empire of the Lands of the South.

The Return of the Sea Peoples

Meanwhile, while the Vietnamese were completing this long march to the south, covering more than six hundred miles and some centuries, and then returning – at the expense of Cambodia – to meet their Thai cousins, who had carried out a similar journey but had come under Indian influence on the way, new sea peoples were appearing who were shortly to turn Indo-

61   62

63

china upside down. First there were the Arabs, coming from India to trade, and then the Indians converted to Islam, who settled in the south of the Malay peninsula and established modest sultanates at least as early as the 14th century. But though they were able to spread the power of Allah throughout almost the whole of Indonesia and as far as the last groups of Chams who still survived on the coasts of Annam, they could make no headway farther north or encroach on Buddhist Siam.

They had, in any event, no time to make further progress; for they were supplanted by other seafarers, coming from still farther west and no less greedy for spices and gold. In 1511 Albuquerque captured Malacca and with it gained control of the sea routes to the East Indies. In the first half of the 16th century merchants, missionaries and soldiers of fortune – often hardly to be distinguished from one another – reached Siam, Burma, Cambodia and Vietnam. But their main interest was in the islands, which were richer in exotic produce; and Indonesia, along with the Philippines, came under the control first of the Spaniards and Portuguese and later of the Dutch. Then the British became masters of India and sought to outflank the Dutch trade routes farther to the north. Accordingly they extended a line of staging posts to the East. In 1786 they were at Penang; in 1819 Raffles founded Singapore; and in 1825 the Straits Settlements were brought under the Viceroy of India.

Burma was the first country to come under pressure from British India, since it was in direct contact with India in Arakan. After a skirmish in 1824 which gave them Arakan, Mergui and Tavoy the British occupied the whole of the Delta in 1852, and finally took Mandalay and the north in 1885. Simultaneously the French were trying to secure a staging post on the route to China. They bombarded Tourane in 1858, took Saigon in 1859, then Cochinchina (1867), and finally the whole of Vietnam (1883). In 1863 Cambodia had appealed for French protection against Siam. In 1893 Auguste Pavie won over Laos. Only Siam escaped conquest – in spite of an attempted French establishment in 1687 to support the missionaries – by virtue of its policy of maintaining the balance between rival contenders, as well as its geographical position as a buffer state between the two great European powers, who found it convenient in this way to avoid further temptations.

And since we are at liberty to reflect on the great rhythms in the history of man, we may note finally that this great movement from the West by way of India and the Indian Ocean was soon to be followed by a move southward by Japan and then China, maintaining into our own day the two-way flow which has marked the history of Indochina from time immemorial.

THE DISCOVERY OF INDOCHINA

IV

Although when the first Europeans landed in Indochina in the 16th century some of the Indochinese states were still developing and expanding, the civilisations of Indochina and the arts which gave them expression were already some way past their peak. At first, however, contacts with Europeans were merely episodic and had no significant political effects. At this stage they left no mark on history: their consequences did not appear until three centuries later[36].

Nor did these contacts lead to an increase in men's knowledge of other lands, as did the first contacts with India, China, and even America. It is true that a few enquiring minds sought to comprehend the new discoveries, a few daring adventurers tried to carve out empires for themselves; but all alike failed in their attempts at conquest, as in their effort to convey knowledge to the people of Europe. If we had to assess the importance of Indochina to Europe at this period, therefore, the answer would be simple: absolutely nil. And if the question were put the other way round the answer would be the same. We must, however, note the main stages in the development of understanding, for they prepared the way for the later discovery of Indochina which concerns us here. The ancient geographers, drawing on the scholarship of Alexandria which had known Asia through the commercial traffic between Rome and India, mentioned an *India extra Gangem* and its principal port of Kattigara[37]; but these were no more than names. It is to Marco Polo that we owe, among so many other things, the first mention of Burma, which was described to him by officials of the Great Khan, and of Champa, which he skirted on his return voyage of 1285. A few travellers followed him to Burma, including the Venetian merchant Nicolo di Conti in 1435[38]. But as the maps of the period show, Indochina was still a *terra incognita ubi sunt leones*.

The quest for spices led to the first continuous relationship with the Far East. Cut off by the Turkish occupation from the whole of the eastern arc of the Mediterranean, the Genoese and Portuguese and Spaniards found their own ways round the obstacles – some to the south round Africa, others to the west by discovering America. As early as 1492 the Malay Peninsula is shown on Martin Behaim's globe, though perhaps on the basis of theory rather than observation, and Magellan's voyage round the world allowed Ribeiro after 1522 to give at last a first sketch of the whole globe. It was not until 1527, however, that the principal states of Indochina – or at least their names – began to appear on the portulans. Meanwhile Vasco da Gama's scouts had reached Malacca in 1508, and in July 1511 Albuquerque established himself there. Thereafter regular trading contacts were rapidly developed between India and Indochina and extended to China, the Philippines, and finally Japan. Albuquerque sent ambassadors to Siam, where they heard about Cambodia. Ludovico di Varthema travelled in 1505–1506 to Tenasserim, and was able to give a reasonably good account of it. In 1516 Fernão Perez de Andrade reached Tonkin. The *Suma orientale* of Tomé Pires (1515) gives us an idea of what Indochina then meant to Europe.

The missionaries soon followed, and their stories were often more detailed. The Dominican Gaspar da Cruz passed through Cambodia in 1555 on his way to China and stayed at the court, of which he gives us some account. He was followed by other Dominicans and then by Franciscans, who sought without much success to establish themselves in the country. The missionaries in turn were followed by bands of enterprising Portuguese and Spanish adventurers who set out in the closing years of the century to conquer the land in the name of the Governor of the Philippines. They were wiped out, and their defeat meant also the end of the missions. Nevertheless these events gave a Portuguese friar, Antonio de la Magdalena, the opportunity about 1585–1589 to visit Angkor, where the Cambodian king had re-established himself. He gave an excellent description of it, which was used by Diogo do Couto, the great Portuguese historian, but by some mischance remained unpublished, so that Angkor, instead of becoming known at this early period, sank back into oblivion[39]. It must be said, however, that if we read these official Portuguese chroniclers we see how little they really knew of these countries, which were of interest to them only for the resources they contained. Mention must also be made here – as the first sign of literary interest in the exotic atmosphere of Indochina – of Camoens, who was shipwrecked in 1560 at the mouths of the Mekong and recounted the incident in his *Lusiads*. The curiosity of the West was no stronger in Tonkin, where it was claimed that the Jesuits had preached the Gospel as early as 1533, or in Siam, where João de Barros mentions in his *Decades* the "pagodas which house Buddhas". More information was gleaned by travellers in Burma, where Western penetration was deeper: so much so that Philip de Brito, a Portuguese soldier of fortune, made himself king at Syriam from 1602 to 1613. There was also, for example, Cesare Frederici, who spent some time there in 1569; and Ralph Fitch, who was there in 1587–1588 and describedthe Shwe Dagon: "...Dogonne... of a woonderfull bignesse, and all gilded from the foot to the toppe... It is the fairest place, as I suppose, that is in the world"[40].

In 1596 J. H. van Linschoten published his *Itinerario... naer Oost ofte Portugaels Indien*, which revealed the secrets of the sea routes so jealously guarded by the Portuguese and opened the way for the "gold rush" by the men of northern Europe towards the riches – often imaginary – of eastern Asia. In a very short time the power of Portugal declined, and it had practically disappeared by 1650; and the Spaniards were boxed up in their possessions in the Philippines, which they could reach only from California across the Pacific. Simultaneously the missionaries were pursuing their efforts, though with so little success that they had in the end to confine themselves to China. The West reaped the benefit, however, in their accounts – often useful and workmanlike – which were summarised in the *Tableau de l'Asie* (1655) which Chaulmer based on their letters. In particular it was they who introduced Tonkin to the West. A Jesuit mission was established at Fai-fo in 1615, and Father de Rhodes, who was there from 1624 to 1645, produced the first Annamite dictionary, and with it established the transcription of this language in Latin characters. The works of C. Borri (1631),

Father Cardim (1645), J. B. Tavernier (1667), who had not been to Tonkin but got his information from his brother Daniel, and Father Tissanier (1663) constitute a considerable stock of information, particularly on local religions. On the basis of this material the British, who traded in this area up to the end of the 17th century, compiled a number of interesting accounts, like those of Samuel Baron (1687) and William Dampier (1688).

But though the Dutch and the British established trading posts in Burma, Malaya, Siam and Cambodia this was only a marginal activity for them, and they did not penetrate into these countries in the full sense of the term. One journey may be mentioned because it is the first known; that of the Batavian merchant Gerit van Wuijsthoff to Laos in 1641. In 1658 the Society for Foreign Missions of Paris began to operate in those regions which had been assigned to it, concentrating particularly on Siam. The extraordinary success of a Greek adventurer, Constant Phaulkon, who had become all-powerful at court, led to a Siamese embassy to Louis XIV in 1684 under the aegis of the missionaries, and this had its counterpart in 1685 in the celebrated mission of the Chevalier de Chaumont and the Abbé de Choisy. The French military intervention which followed these exchanges ended catastrophically in 1688. But in the flood of pamphlets and more substantial accounts to which these events gave rise we find some important contributions to our knowledge of Siam, beginning with the description by La Loubère (1691). Also worth noting is the passage in which the Jesuit Father Bouvet gives, in 1687, the first Western comment on the archaeology of this country: "Not one of these pagodas but is entirely painted within, and is accompanied without by a number of carefully wrought pyramids of different sizes... The body of these pyramids, as of the others, is ornamented with a kind of architectural order which has some resemblance to our own, but which being more charged with sculptures, and lacking the simplicity and the proportions of ours, has not the same beauty, at least in our eyes which are not yet accustomed to it"[41].

It is a curious fact, not yet sufficiently explained, that the 18th century saw a very distinct decline in European enterprises in Indochina. No doubt the British, French and Dutch were too fully occupied in India to have time for these other areas which had not lived up to their expectations of trade, and which were in any event torn at this period by implacable strife. A further factor was the expulsion of the missionaries from Vietnam in 1750. The British, however, continued to push their trading posts farther into Malaya and Burma; and the French sought to counter them by establishing a base at Syriam from which, with the help of the north-eastern monsoon, a squadron could control the whole of the Bay of Bengal. But the century has little to show in the way of serious studies of these countries; perhaps the only one worth mentioning is Father Köffler's account of Tonkin. In amusing contrast we have the great vogue which swept Europe, under the influence of the *philosophes*, for "Tonkinese Anecdotes", "Siamese Anecdotes", and so on, in which, after the fashion of Montesquieu's *Lettres Persanes*, criticisms of current European governments and manners were cloaked in an exotic disguise. A more serious note is sometimes found in writings of this type: for example the *Voyages d'un Philosophe* (1768) by the "physiocrat" Pierre Poivre, which contains the first explanation of the power of Angkor based on the development of agriculture. Apart from geography – the maps of Indochina by d'Anville (1737) and d'Après (1745) are almost perfect – no branch of human knowledge had collected the basic material about these areas. The natural sciences, however, were beginning to discover the immense scope which they offered to their enquiries[42].

It is not until the turn of the century that European awareness of Indochina becomes more precise. Having got rid of the French and gained control over the Dutch, the British were politically and economically ready to advance from their base in India. A man of genius, Raffles, provided them with the means to do so by the foundation of Singapore in 1819 and the temporary occupation of Java, where he was to discover Borobudur. With the activity of a conqueror he combined a gift for the natural sciences and the vision of a historian – so much so that he planned to establish in Singapore a school of translators whose task it would be to "collect the scattered remains of the literature of these countries"[43]. His lieutenants compiled the first monographs on the area, like Crawfurd's *Indian Archipelago*, published in 1820.

Meanwhile in Burma Dr. Burney had begun, in 1825, his quest for the historical sources, and the American missionaries, led by A. Judson who arrived in 1813, were transcribing the native language and literature. Then there was a whole series of scientific voyages – Bougainville in 1825, Laplace in the *Favorite* in 1830, Vaillant in the *Bonite* in 1836. In Vietnam the efforts of Mgr Pigneau de Béhaine had succeeded in 1787 in opening up the country to the missionaries and to the French officers who had come to help Gia Long in his reconquest; and they in turn reawakened French interest in the country. The substantial body of information which these developments made available enabled Europeans to form a general picture of this part of the world. It is worth mentioning also that we owe the very name of Indochina, thought of surprisingly late in the day, to one of these scholars – Malte-Brun, who used it in the fourth volume of his *Précis de géographie universelle* (1813)[44]. The enterprise was made easier by the fact that India and China were now being systematically studied. Taking as his model the Asiatic Society of Bengal, Renan had founded in 1822 the Société Asiatique of Paris. By 1814 Sanskrit and Chinese were being taught at the Collège de France, and the School of Oriental Languages had been established twenty years earlier, in 1795. The religions of India were unravelled, and the accounts of Chinese ambassadors to the Southern Seas were discovered. In 1819 Abel Rémusat translated the account of Chou Ta-kuan, who visited Angkor in 1296 and left a lively description of it which is still an indispensable source for students.

The movement gained additional impetus when European embassies were sent to the kingdoms of Indochina, for Western curiosity was doubly

81, 82, 83, 84, 85→

stimulated by political objectives and by the desire for knowledge. Crawfurd, sent on a mission to the court of Ava in 1827, revealed the art of Burma,
and noted that "the building of a temple among the Burmans is not only
a work of piety, but the chief species of luxury and ostentation, in which
those who have become possessed of wealth either by industry or extortion,
are permitted to indulge" – a shrewd observation which also explains many
aspects of Angkor. At this period too a number of standard works which
are still consulted were written, like the books on Burma by Father Sanger-
mano (1833), on Siam by Mgr Pallegoix (1854), and on Cochinchina by
J. B. Chaigneau (1820)[45].

In short, a new world had emerged, as Chateaubriand says in his *Memoirs*,
in words which, though rhetorical, are not without nobility: "Then the
whole surface of the globe was changed: a new face of nature appeared;
the curtain which had for thousands of centuries covered part of the earth
was raised, and there was revealed to men the country of the sun, the place
from which it rose each morning... There was exposed to view the wise
and splendid East, whose mysterious history was mingled with the journeys
of Pythagoras, the conquests of Alexander, and the memories of the Crusa-
des, and whose perfumes were wafted across the fields of Arabia and the
seas of Greece."

Bayon, Angkor. North front. Sandstone; 140×160 m. at the base; total height 43 m. Bayon style; beginning of 13th century.

INVENTORY OF INDOCHINA

V

The Quest for Knowledge

Colonial conquest was at the origin of the systematic study of Indochina. Political necessity, the attraction of the exotic missionary zeal, the desire to fit all this new information into the general picture of the human sciences which were growing up – the motives are of little importance now that we have the results.

As the name it had newly been given made clear, Indochina was approached by way of what was already known about India and China. In consequence Indochinese studies perhaps tended at first to be limited by this approach, and were inclined to regard the countries with which they were concerned as merely minor provinces of these two great centres of civilisation. Very soon, however, exploration and discovery were to reveal all the wealth they contained, and to make good their claim to an independent existence.

The archaeological heritage of Burma was revealed in 1858 when Sir Henry Yule published an account of his mission to the court of Ava. After the conquest administrators and shrewd soldiers sought to find out more about their new subjects; and in 1883 Phayre published the first substantial history of the country. In Cambodia discoveries no less remarkable were attracting even more attention. In 1860 the French naturalist Henri Mouhot arrived at Angkor. He was not the first visitor, but his enthusiastic articles in the great European newspapers revealed to the world the city which had been thought to be lost for ever. "Ruins so imposing," he cried, "the fruit of such prodigious labour that on seeing them we are seized with the profoundest admiration... ruins which can stand comparison with our finest churches, and which surpass in grandeur all that the art of the Greeks and the Romans ever achieved"[46]. Soon afterwards Mouhot was to disappear in the Laotian jungle, but he will always deserve credit as the founder of the legend of Angkor. In 1866 the Scottish explorer John Thomson took the first photographs of Angkor and was able to divine the cosmic symbolism, according to the Hindu system, of Angkor Vat[47]. As early as 1863 the German orientalist A. Bastian had discovered the Indian origin of the religion and the script of Angkor. Doudart de Lagrée visited Angkor in 1866 and again in 1867 on his celebrated surveying expedition on the Mekong. He died of exhaustion in Yunnan, but his assistants continued the task. Francis Garnier caused translations to be made of the Cambodian royal chronicles and of Wuijsthoff's journey to Laos. Louis Delaporte returned on a mission in 1873 and, after visiting the principal Khmer sites, took back to France a quantity of sculptures and casts which aroused interest in the first Indochinese museum in the Trocadéro in Paris. He also produced the first general study of Khmer art. The Cham monuments were discovered in 1885, and Charles Lemire found some Cham remains at Tourane in 1892.

Dr. Harmand, the indefatigable explorer of Cambodia and Laos between 1875 and 1877, had sent rubbings of inscriptions to the great Dutch orientalist Hendrick Kern, who recognised them as Sanskrit texts. Auguste Barth, the leading French authority on Indian studies – soon joined by A. Bergaigne – began the systematic publication of the Sanskrit texts of Cambodia and Champa, which yielded dates and other historical information. Moura, French Resident in Cambodia and one of those scholarly sailors who have contributed so much to knowledge, produced in his *Royaume du Cambodge* (1883) the first general history of the country. His successor Etienne Aymonier sent rubbings and other material to Paris; then, having learned Sanskrit, produced the first translations of the ancient Khmer language and of the Champa texts. After travelling from end to end of the country he published his *Cambodge* (1900), a compendium which brought together the impressive results achieved by a whole generation of strikingly fruitful research[48].

The scale of discovery, the realisation – as the administration of the country became established – of the task that lay ahead, and the progress and the requirements of Oriental studies in Europe, now an accepted discipline, all pointed to the necessity of establishing permanent bodies to carry on the work; for it was now beyond the resources of individual amateurs or even of learned societies, like the Société des Études Indochinoises which had been founded at Saigon in 1865. In British India the movement had been begun by J. Fergusson and A. Cunningham in 1845; it was continued by Lord Minto, who restored the Taj Mahal, and above all by Lord Curzon, who in 1900 gave a fresh impulsion to the Archaeological Survey of India, declaring: "It is ...equally our duty to dig and discover, to classify, re-produce and describe, to copy and decipher, and to cherish and conserve". In 1899 the Archaeological Department of Burma was founded and began to restore the temples of Pagan; and at the same time the Rangoon Museum was established. The great French Indianists Barth, Bréal and Bergaigne secured the establishment in 1898 of the Ecole Française d'Extrême-Orient at Saigon, with the task of studying the past of the country within the framework of Oriental studies. Paul Doumer transferred it to Hanoi, where he also founded the Geographical and Geological Services; and it was later to become the Directorate of Museums and Historical Monuments of Indo-china[49]. Henceforth the researches of the learned bodies of Europe, of these new institutions, and fortunately also of many individual enquirers, could be systematically planned. The results achieved can be considered under a number of main headings dealing with particular fields or areas of study.

Prehistoric Studies

Although a logical approach would have required the contrary, prehistoric studies are in fact the youngest and most backward branch of Indochinese research[50], just as in Europe they are the most recent chapter in our know-ledge of the past. The reasons for this are apparent: prehistoric remains, with the exception of megaliths, are not easily seen on the ground, and are found only by systematic research. As we have seen, moreover, the soil and climate of the Indochinese peninsula are particularly unfavourable to the preservation of remains: stone and pottery are almost the only things that survive. The earliest inhabited areas – that is, the more accessible upland areas, the coasts, and the shores of the lakes – are now abandoned and covered by vegetation, or have been profoundly modified by man and by nature, by erosion, alluvial deposits, or changes in sea-level.

As might be expected, it was the geologists who first took an interest in the oldest human remains. Their researches were particularly successful in two areas. One was Tonkin, where the Geological Service of Indochina was established in 1899. The other was Malaya – perhaps because British traditions favoured this field of study, or perhaps because the absence of visible monuments, at any rate until recent years, stimulated the search for buried remains. Samrong Sen, in Cambodia, was one of the first prehistoric sites studied in Indochina. Roques drew attention to it in 1874; objects from here were published by Corre in 1879; and in 1887 the industrious Ludovic Jammes seems to have attempted here what others attempted at Glozel and Piltdown, but with less success and less glory than they.

In fact the geologists Patte and Mansuy can be considered the founders of Indochinese prehistory, along with their disciples like Father de Pirey and above all Madeleine Colani, who later became a member of the Ecole Française d'Extrême-Orient and established this discipline there. This tradition of geologist-prehistorians was brilliantly continued by E. Saurin, to whom we owe the essentials of our stratigraphy, our palaeontological basis and our terminology.

As early as 1906 Mansuy had been able to define the Bacsonian on the basis of his field surveys, particularly at Phu-lang-tuong and Lang-son. Madeleine Colani extended these researches, discovering in 1923 the cave of Lang-cuom, which was remarkably rich in human remains; and her excavations of 1927 to 1928 enabled her to define the Hoabinian. Then, indefatigably, she extended her researches to Cam-mon, Tran-ninh and Hua P'an.

Identical horizons were later defined by reference to these categories, notably by F. Sarrasin in Siam in 1933, by Collings at Kota Tampan (North Perak) in 1938, and by J. Coggin Brown and T. C. Morris in Burma from 1935 to 1938. The Neolithic industries, which had been known since the discovery of Samrong Sen, were found in increasing numbers in Tonkin, in Annam with the kitchen middens of Da-but (Thanh-hoa) and Bau-tro which were excavated from 1924 to 1925, and then at Sa-huynh which was re-examined in 1933 by van Stein-Callenfels. The pace increased in 1937–1938, with work by J. G. Andersson and M. Colani at Baie d'Along, E. Saurin in the cave of Nhommalat (Cam-mon), O. Janse at the Ile de la Tortue (Bien-hoa), and P. Lévy at Mlu Prei (Kompong Thom). The war interrupted this promising work, the true beginning of Indochinese pre-history.

In 1930, too, there had been noted at Xa-cat (Cochinchina) the first "Moi forts", the importance of which is considered below; and already they were compared with identical remains at K'orat and Utaradit in Thailand. In Malaya, where the first remains had aroused the interest of Ivor Evans at the end of last century, we owe most of our knowledge to the excellent and substantial works of M. W. F. Tweedie, and it is due to him that studies in this field are so advanced and so coherent. The megaliths of Perak had, of course, been noted very early. The "jars" of Tran-ninh had also attracted attention at least as early as 1909. They were finally published by Madeleine Colani; and in 1927 J. Bouchot excavated the megalithic burial chamber at Xuan-loc, proving that this civilisation extended well beyond the centre of Laos.

But it was the Bronze Age remains in Thanh-hoa that aroused the greatest interest. The first discoveries were made in 1919, and the collection formed by Col. d'Argencé, later acquired by the Hanoi Museum, contained many specimens. The carrying out of large-scale public works at Thanh-hoa led to so many finds that the Ecole Française d'Extrême-Orient realised that if earth-moving on this scale had to be done it might as well be done by them. The work was entrusted to a technical assistant, whose most striking qualification was his abundant energy. He set to work on Da-but in 1925, and then concentrated his attention on Dong-son. However splendid the isolation of French archaeology at this period and in this area, it could not indefinitely ignore the criticisms aroused by this hunt for treasure trove: in 1934, therefore, a Swedish prehistorian, Olav Janse, was called in, and worked mainly at Dong-son from 1934 to 1939[51]. He introduced order into the researches, drew up plans in at least two dimensions, and collected, identified and studied the finds: all of which was quite new and finally made it possible to get a coherent picture of the Dongsonian. Simultaneously parallel material was being studied in Malaya, and comparisons were being made with the bronzes discovered at Samrong Sen and in the Plain of Jars. Meanwhile, too, prehistoric studies were making remarkable progress in China and Indonesia, providing the basis for wider syntheses.

For this work in the field was accompanied by the first theoretical models designed to interpret them, or at least to fit them into a rational scheme with some appearance of reality. By a curious paradox which is not peculiar to Indochinese prehistory, the main work on these theories was done by men who had not only never worked in Indochina but were for long to remain ignorant of it. It is true that they were looking at the material as part of a wider picture, extending from China to Indonesia. In some ways this was a good thing, for otherwise it would have been impossible to understand Indochina; but it was also a bad thing in that the precariousness of most of the data was never sufficiently appreciated by these scholars.

In 1902 F. Heger studied the bronze drums, which from 1883 onwards had been appearing in European collections, and agreed with de Groot in

87   86   88

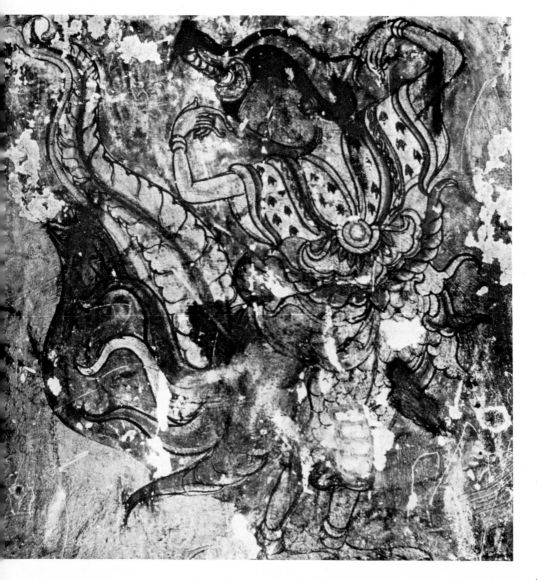

deriving them from southern China. In 1929 Victor Goloubew, who had been following the work at Thanh-hoa, published his *L'Age du bronze au Tonkin*[52], the first comprehensive treatment of the new discoveries. Although he was quite without any stratigraphical basis and depended on typological and stylistic comparisons which were often tenuous, he usefully brought out the Chinese influences. Apart from this Goloubew's main contribution was – following a brilliant intuition of Edouard Huber's – to interpret the scenes represented on the drums in the light of ethnography, particularly of material on the Dyaks. Even allowing for the chronological hiatus and the objections in principle to this method, it must be said that these theories, recently supported by Jean Przyluski among others, are still an essential contribution.

The general picture of man's beginnings in South-East Asia was very usefully studied at the first Congress of Far Eastern Prehistory which was held at Hanoi in 1931. This congress also led to the formation of an association which was given a fresh lease of life in 1953 and has since played a fundamental part in these studies[53]. But it was a brilliant Austrian prehistorian, Robert von Heine-Geldern, who first arranged all the known facts into a series of remarkable working hypotheses, published from 1932 onwards[54]. His ideas have been used by so many later students that they need not be summarised here: they are the basis of the brief account of the Neolithic given in this book, and we shall consider below how far they have been outdated and how they stand up to the latest discoveries. It is right, however, to stress the importance of these writings, and also his daring hypothesis on the origin of the Dongsonian. According to Heine-Geldern, this is to be related to the Thraco-Cimmerians of the Hallstatt culture settled south of the Danube. He suggests that when were driven out of this area by the Scythians they crossed the whole of central Asia to emerge in China, where they destroyed the civilisation of the Chou; then one wave travelled on through the south-west of the country into Tonkin, where they mingled with the native races.

Finally in 1942 a decisive advance was marked by the publication of a study of the Dongsonian by the eminent philologist Bernard Karlgren. Karlgren also helped to establish the chronology of archaic Chinese bronzes. Basing himself on this experience, he brought together an impressive number of stylistic parallels buttressed by Chinese historical data, and showed that the plastic sources of the bronzes of Thanh-hoa were to be sought in the Chinese style of the Warring States, from the 4th–3th centuries B.C.[55].

Khmer Studies

We have already referred to the beginnings of Khmer epigraphy, and need only note that it has continued to make progress, thanks in particular to the work of Louis Finot and George Coedès, and that as a result all the known texts – about a thousand – have now been published and translated. Simultaneously Paul Pelliot was drawing together all that the Chinese texts had to say about the Southern Seas, and the Indianists – including, in particular, great authorities like Sylvain Lévi and Alfred Foucher – were making progress in their own field, providing a constant point of reference and a standard for Further India.

In 1900 Lunet de Lajonquière began his inventory of the Khmer monuments under the auspices of the French School: a work outstanding for the speed of its completion, its clarity, and its scale, which has not yet been superseded. At the same time Henri Parmentier was in charge of the archaeological work of the School. In 1907 France compelled Siam to return to Cambodia the provinces of Siemreap and Battambang, which contained Angkor and the principal Khmer monuments. The Angkor Conservancy was at once established and put in charge of Jean Commaille; and when he was murdered on his excavation site in 1916 he was succeeded by Henri Marchal. The first efforts were devoted to the clearing and recording of the temples, a colossal task which in less than twenty years revealed over eight hundred sites and a great wealth of finds *(Plates 116-119)*. In 1916 George Groslier built the Cambodian Museum at Phnom Penh, gathering objects from all over the country to make it the central shrine of Khmer art. Here all the masterpieces from Angkor found a home. The first photographic coverage had been carried out at the Bayon in 1908 by Dufour and Carpeau, then at Angkor Vat and Banteay Chmar *(Plates 39, 129)* on the initiative of Gen. de Beylié; and these, along with the publications, made it possible for students far from Cambodia to become familiar with its arts.

Throughout this first phase the identification and dating of the monuments remained essentially in the hands of the epigraphists. When the texts were the actual foundation inscriptions there was little room for doubt; but some writers felt able to go a stage farther and use this method to link isolated texts with particular buildings which were supposed to correspond to the descriptions given in the texts. Thus the temples of Indravarman and Angkor Vat were dated directly; but it was also suggested, on the basis of a later text, that the Bayon was erected by Yasovarman and was therefore to be dated, along with similar buildings, to about the year 900. These theories were accepted without hesitation even by those responsible for studying the temples on the ground, who were ready to bend their observations to fit the dogmas. Meanwhile no attention was paid to stratigraphic techniques or to the other methods of archaeological investigation which were taken for granted on the sites of Europe and America: not a single excavation was carried out at Angkor until 1953. The material civilisation of the Khmers was for all practical purposes unknown, and the only progress made in this field was the archaeological study by George Groslier of the scenes represented in paintings and carvings.

It was the very considerable achievement of Philippe Stern, an art historian with a remarkable intuitive flair who worked on the material in the Musée Guimet in Paris, to throw doubt on the official chronology. In 1927, with some moral courage, he published a thesis which showed the inconsistency of the very early date accepted for the Bayon and suggested that it should be brought down at least a century later. His work created a considerable stir. George Coedès – his absolute confidence in earlier judgements shaken – went back with remarkable objectivity to the texts and at last restored to Jayavarman VII the monumental buildings which he inspired. Then, thanks to the closest cooperation between the art historians and the epigraphists, the chronology and the stylistic development of the great Khmer temples were rapidly, and this time definitively, established; and in 1939, basing herself on Stern's work, Mme de Coral-Rémusat was able to present the results. With this new perspective the facts fitted more readily into place. Victor Goloubew proved that the Bakheng was the temple built in 900 by Yasovarman in the centre of a town which he saw from an aircraft piloted by L. Terrasson, thus inaugurating one of the most promising developments in the study of Khmer archaeology *(Plates 127, 128, 138)*. In 1935, in the course of a mission to Angkor, Philippe Stern showed the richness of the early periods, particularly on the Kulen, where he cleared a certain number of buildings.

Meanwhile the success achieved in the reconstruction of temples by the Netherlands Indies Archaeological Service in Java was beginning to shake the Angkor Conservancy out of its complacent torpor. Georges Trouvé, who was Conservator from 1931 to 1935[56], began to apply the same techniques on a large scale. His main achievement was a remarkable survey in the course of which he made great numbers of discoveries and in particular established the fundamental importance of irrigation in the Khmer city[57]. Maurice Glaize, who was Conservator from 1937 to 1945, showed robust commonsense in applying the techniques of complete restoration to some of the large complexes of buildings at Angkor, and it is to him that we owe their survival. Finally the work of investigation and preservation was gradually extended to the whole of Cambodia – for example to Asram Maha Rosei, Phnom Chisor, Phnom Bayang, etc. *(Plates 119, 124)*.

With the help of this improved documentation the interpretation of the Khmer monuments in the general context of their civilisation now made considerable progress. From 1927 onwards some Indian scholars, including in particular R. C. Majumdar, were taking an interest in the expansion of the civilisation of their ancestors, bringing to this study an original vision based on an intimate acquaintance with their own tradition – as well as a quite legitimate pride in their past. The Dutch orienta- lists were establishing the funerary character of the monuments of Java and were throwing light on some aspects of the Khmer temples. In 1923 Louis Finot detected the influence of salvationist Buddhism in monuments which were still dated to the 10th century. From 1928 onwards Paul Mus, with his extraordinary understanding of Buddhism, was elucidating the symbolism of the great buil- dings which were now recognised as belonging to the reign of Jaya- varman VII.

As the history of Cambodia was built up on the basis of epigraphy and the archaeology of the monuments it was possible to get a clearer picture of the problems raised by its formation. In 1917 George Coedès showed that Tchen-la was to be localised in the area of Basak, and in 1932 he published the first inscriptions from Fu-nan. As early as 1908-1911 objects and then sites which were probably Khmer, but of a very ancient period, had been found in Cochinchina by Parmentier and Gen. de Beylié. Pierre Dupont discovered at Phnom Da some splendid pieces of statuary which he related, in his excellent historical studies of the 6th to 8th centuries, to the tradition of Fu-nan, and which he published in a work which is a model of exhaustive study *(Plate 18)*. Louis Malleret, director of the Saigon Museum which had been established in 1928 for this new province of archaeology, began his methodical survey, and this led him in 1944 to examine the mounds at Oc-eo which were revealed as a site belonging to the first of the great Indianised empires, Fu-nan, which could thus at last be given a geographi- cal identity *(Plates 15, 16, 17)*.

Cham Studies

Though it may have lacked the glamour of the temples lost in the jungle, and thus – unfairly, in view of its interest and historical importance – failed to attract the same public attention, the study of Cham civilisation is one of the most fascinating chapters in the story of Indochinese studies. Here too, epigraphy provided the guiding thread. Following in the foot stepsof Barth and Bergaigne and the essays of Aymonier and Landes, and using the material contributed by Indonesian studies towards the understanding of the Old Cham language, a number of scholars – L. Finot, G. Coedès, L. Huber and P. Mus – published the Cham texts, which were now well known. Henri Maspéro combed the Chinese histories for material which enabled his brother Georges to produce in 1928 a general history of this civilisation.

One by one the monuments were brought to notice by travellers, and above all by missionaries like Fathers de Pirey, Escalère, Durand and Cadière. A systematic inventory was published by H. Parmentier in 1909, and it was a well deserved tribute to his labours when the museum built at Tourane in 1918 to house the masterpieces of Cham art was given his name. He cleared Po Klaung Garai in 1901, Dong-duong in 1902, and – most important of all – Mi-son from 1903 onwards *(Plates 41, 64)*. He also sought to restore some of these towers which were on the point of collapse; but the restoration of a structure built in brick is an extremely delicate operation, and it cannot be said that the results are particularly successful, even from the point of view of preserving the structure. The survey work was continued by J. Y. Claëys, who in 1927 cleared some interesting sculpture at Tra-kieu and in 1934 made further discoveries at Thap-mam. He also restored the Po Nagar at Nhatrang, the tower of Bang-an, *(Plate 42)* and many buildings at Mi-son.

In establishing the chronology of Cham art scholars got even less help than in Cambodia from inscriptions definitely associated with particular temples.

It was necessary, therefore, to fall back on the purely aesthetic study carried out by Parmentier, who – basing himself on his very personal ideas on "art" and its "evolution" – classified as primitive what was afterwards shown to be late. Here again the error was corrected by Philippe Stern, using the very meagre material available and depending largely on his understanding of its development. His *Art du Champa*, published in 1942, laid down a clear and well reasoned system. Finally, in 1947, R. Stein produced a work which was not perhaps directly in the field of monumental archaeology but was a remarkable example of the archaeological study of the texts: reviewing all the Chinese sources, he laid the definitive foundations of our knowledge of the country and prepared the way for all later field work.

In order to complete the picture of the coastal area of Indochina, where the Indonesian element was predominant, we must mention the Malay Peninsula. As we have seen, the lack of monuments in this area gave a special impetus to prehistoric studies. The few inscriptions known had, however, attracted the attention of James Low in 1857, and they were translated in part by H. Kern and Hultzsch, the great specialist on southern India. Later Coedès, Majumdar, Krom and Vogel successively studied these documents, along with the documents from Indonesia, with the object of establishing the much disputed history of Srivijaya. Unfortunately their work was not confirmed by any systematic archaeological investigations, although the indefatigable Lunet de Lajonquière had drawn attention in 1907 to the promising possibilities at Ch'aiya and Kra *(Plates 8, 26, 28, 30)*. It was not until 1935 that the work of Dr. Quaritch Wales brought a certain amount of new information. But Quaritch Wales was chiefly concerned to establish "the Indians' road to Angkor", and tended to place more reliance on material which confirmed – or appeared to confirm – his theories. He must at least, however, be allowed the credit of having demonstrated the possibilities of this area. At the end of the day it is only because of the careful and methodical work of the prehistorians that we have a few Indian objects attributed with certainty to particular sites.

Burmese Studies

In Burma the epigraphical sources were at first extremely difficult, and students had to begin with the historical chronicles. But these did not go back beyond the foundation of Pagan, or where they did were a mingling of legendary traditions and historical reminiscences. It was necessary, therefore, to go back to the lapidary inscriptions. As early as 1860 Harwell had studied the Mon language. In 1892 Forchhammer published Burmese and Pali texts. In 1905 the excavations at Prome yielded Pyu inscriptions which were not deciphered by Blagden until 1911 with the help of the quadrilingual inscription of Myazedi, dated to 1100, which contained parallel texts in Mon, Pali and Burmese.

Charles Duroiselle, Professor of Pali at Rangoon, played a fundamental role in the archaeological investigations. At first counsellor to Taw Sein Ko and later superintendent of the Archaeological Survey, he began investigations at Prome in 1905 along with Gen. de Beylié and a mission from the Ecole Française d'Extrême-Orient. He then (1907) turned to Pagan, where he identified the Mon *jatakas* of Petleik and the Ananda temple, on which he published an excellent monograph *(Plates 72, 73, 74)*. In 1916 he discovered the frescoes of the temples of Minnanthu and recognised the complex Buddhist traditions which had inspired them *(Plate 93)*. In 1921–1922 he carried out successful surveys in Arakan and then returned to Prome, where work was to continue until 1936. At the same time the Archaeological Survey – which had taken some Burmese on to its staff and had thus given them a passionate concern for their own past – was restoring the great buildings, starting with the palaces of Mandalay in 1919 and then going on to the temples of Pagan. In some cases they were anticipated by the monks, whose zeal – comprehensive and somewhat over-possessive – led them to undertake lavish whitewashing or regilding operations, or in some cases to adopt the alternative solution of applying a fresh layer of brick or stucco. Finally the indefatigable H. G. Luce and U Pe Maung Tin were building up

103, 104, 105, 106→

102

101

the history of the country as material became available from excavation or from their systematic survey of the Chinese and Siamese sources. But although, with the help of the historical chronicles, the dating of the monuments from the foundation of Pagan onwards is relatively easy, it has not led to any systematic stylistic study, in spite of Le May's articles on the sculpture.

The Thai Countries

At first Thai studies did not attract a great deal of attention, and there were no permanent research institutions devoted to them. In 1884 S. Beal, publishing the travels of the Chinese Buddhist pilgrim Hiuen-Tsiang, proposed to locate Dvaravati in southern Siam, and received support from P. Pelliot, who already sensed that it was a Mon country. Then in 1919 G. Coedès published inscriptions discovered in this area which were in fact in Mon. The Thai texts, for which a Royal Library had been established in 1881, were deciphered successively by Father W. Schmidt, Bradley, Petit-Huguenin, L. Finot and G. Coedès.

Lunet de Lajonquière drew up the first inventory of the monuments of Siam, mostly built by the Khmers, and this was kept up to date by the devoted labours of Eric Seidenfaden. The Siam Society, which had been in existence since 1904, played a fundamental part in Siamese studies; but it was not until 1925 that an Archaeological Survey was established. It began by clearing and protecting Wat Mahathat at Lop'buri and Wat Sri Sarapath and Budhaisavan at Ayuthya *(Plates 98, 103)*. Meanwhile George Coedès, then attached to it as an adviser, was publishing the first systematic collection of Siamese inscriptions. In all its enterprises a decisive part was played by Prince Damrong, to whose energy Siam owed the recovery of its past. In 1926 the Royal Library, the National Museum and the Archaeological

Survey were brought together in a Directorate of the Arts, which supported and strengthened them. In 1927 G. Coedès and Manfredi recognised
remains at P'ong Tuk *(Plate 9)* which seemed to belong to the art of
Dvaravati. In 1929 J. Y. Claëys surveyed the whole country and drew up a
first descriptive inventory of Thai buildings, which is still of value. In 1935
Quaritch Wales carried out further excavations at P'ong Tuk and in the Sri
T'ep area, where he had no difficulty in identifying further landmarks on
the road to Angkor. Finally in 1939–1940 Pierre Dupont cleared the large
brick buildings near Nak'on Pathom *(Plates 106, 115)*, collecting an abundant store of decorative plaster work. It was not until 1943, however, that
two silver coins were found here inscribed with the very name of Dvaravati
which the shrewd intuitions of the historians had already assigned to the
area. Throughout this whole period the main studies of art history in the
field had been those of R. S. Le May, to whom we owe the first classification of Thai Buddhist sculpture, a work which still retains some value.

Laos, buried inland, received much less attention. Auguste Pavie, the
remarkable man who won over the country in the course of a series of
journeys carried out between 1876 and 1895, gathered a first collection of
documents, and this was supplemented by L. Finot in 1917 on the basis of
a careful examination of the texts. Following in Lunet de Lajonquière's
footsteps, H. Parmentier studied the pagodas of the country, and drew up
an inventory which is of particular value because practically all the monuments he describes have unfortunately disappeared since then. The architects
of the School, however, did what they could to save them: in 1914 Batteur
restored the That Si Chanand at Vientiane, and in 1930 Fombertaux began
work on Th'at Luang in the same town. Then in 1936 work was be gunat
Vat P'ra Keo under the direction of Tiao Souvanna Phouma *(Plate 105)*.
In 1937 J. Y. Claëys discovered ancient walls round Vientiane in an aerial
survey and demonstrated the possibilities of this method in the valley of the
Mekong. Finally P. Lévy used archaeological remains to trace the history
of the introduction of Buddhism at Luang P'ra Bang.

Vietnamese Studies

It is traditional to reproach the archaeologists with neglecting Vietnam. As we have seen, this is entirely false so far as prehistory is concerned; and moreover it is an empty reproach, for the country is particularly rich in literary traditions. In any event there has in fact always been a fair amount of research and investigation in this area.

Chéon and Landes were the founders of Vietnamese philology, and the language was taught at Paris as early as 1896. With the help of Chinese the texts presented little difficulty. G. Dumoutier, the government interpreter, realised when he arrived at Hanoi in 1886 the importance of the Chinese tombs in the history of the country, and the interest of ancient cities like Co-loa and Hoa-lu, and he arranged for Vildieu to make a record of the pagodas of the capital. In 1914 was founded the Association des Amis du Vieux-Hué, the moving spirits of which were the great figure of Père Cadière and other talented scholars; the Association's *Bulletin* is an inexhaustible mine of information. Cadière's contributions included a study of the Wall of Dong-hoi which is an excellent example of historical archaeology.

From 1913 onwards the Chinese tombs were beginning to be emptied of their contents – at Quang-yen and Bac-ninh by H. Parmentier and later by Pajot, at Lac-y (Vinh-yen) by Claëys and then by Olav Janse. The architects of the French School, de Mecquenem and Demasur, made a record of the imperial tombs at Hué, and Charles Batteur did likewise for the *dinh* of Dinh-bang (Bac-ninh). Batteur then restored the Temple of Literature and the Pagoda of the Single Pillar at Hanoi. (The latter was unfortunately destroyed in 1954). From 1937, under the direction of L. Bezacier, the work of restoration proceeded systematically and was extended to the whole country – including, for example, the Ninh-phuc pagoda at But-thap, the Van-phuc pagoda at Phat-tich, and Gia Long's Can-than Palace at Hué.

The plans drawn in the course of this work were later published, and are a model of their kind. The work of restoration also involved the excavation of earlier remains which confirmed the chronology of Vietnamese art; and methodical surveys led to the discovery of important monuments whose existence had not hitherto been suspected, such as the tower-*stupa* of Binh-son (1932) and the frescoes in the cave of Thien-khe (1941). Aerial surveys had also made their contribution, revealing the line of the wall erected by the Mac dynasty against the Chinese and the earthworks of Co-loa.

This brief summary, tedious though it may seem with its dry but necessary list of names and dates, seeks to show the immense progress that has been made since the enquiries of the dilettantes of the 18th century. In 1861 Barthélémy Saint-Hilaire was able to declare, with the serene confidence which always marks the statement of an ineptitude: "With the possible exception of Burma, all the countries of Transgangetic India – Tonkin, Cochinchina, Cambodia, Laos, Pegu and Arakan – are scarcely worth the attention of history"[58]. Less than a century later, by the eve of the second World War which was to throw Indochina into turmoil, two generations of scholars had built an imposing edifice and enriched history with a fascinating new chapter. The road had not been an easy one, and some of those who travelled it had sacrificed their lives on the way. But though the names of most of these men are now forgotten it is by their efforts that cities like Angkor and Pagan have at last been brought back to life.

INDOCHINA: THE SUMMING UP

VI

We have presented a brief archaeological inventory of Indochina, and have shown the immense labour that went to its compilation. It might reasonably be supposed, therefore, that these conclusions have been finally established and give a fair picture of the history of the areas. But this, alas, is not so. If we now set out to cast doubt on some of these ideas, the contradiction is only apparent. It is true that if we consider what was known a century ago, or the theories then in favour, we see what vast strides have been made since then. It is true also that we can point to an impressive body of established facts. But it is still not so detailed, so exact, or indeed so accurate, as is sometimes claimed. The material we have is only a part, and in some respects only a tiny part, of what remains to be discovered. As a result the historical record is fragmentary and all too often unreliable.

Nor is it from sheer delight in contradiction, or from hostility to an earlier generation or doctrine, that we seek to revise earlier theories. The reader must have been struck by the small number of workers who have been active in this field. Their achievement is all the greater for this, and to suggest that they did not do everything is not to diminish that achievement. The disciplines with which we are concerned are all young: the present generation is only the third, and it is the only one to have had the advantage of a properly organised training, thanks to the labours of those who have gone before. There are fashions in research, trends which differ from one country to another and from one time to another; and there are tensions.

But these confrontations, these collisions, these changes are valuable if they lead us to probe the foundations, to examine and consolidate the sound parts, to understand and imitate the earlier examples which remain valid, to discover the gaps and seek to fill them; and having thus established a solid base, to advance from there. If we did not do this the paths opened up by the first explorers as they pushed their way into the unknown would become no better than ruts. If we did not do this our progress would be merely vain repetition, or an embroidery of useless detail: wasted effort when so much remains to be done. Let us profit, therefore, from the fact that, in the words of the scholiast Bernard of Chartres, "we are no more than dwarfs; but, perched on the shoulders of our masters, we cannot fail to see farther than they"; and let us attempt to sum up, under a few main heads, the knowledge we have gained[59].

The Problem of Origins

Within the last few years the prehistory of Indochina has made remarkable progress: understandably enough, for it had most ground to make up. It benefited, in the first place, from the discoveries in China and Indonesia and the works of synthesis which they made possible. The improvement in methods of excavation and of examining material with the help of an elaborate network of laboratories, and the appearance of techniques of absolute dating, have given a fresh impetus to researches which were much in need of it. But prehistory has to base itself on facts, and too little reliable data had been collected before the war to offer much scope for fresh theoretical approaches; and unfortunately conditions since the war have not been favourable to investigations in the field.

Nevertheless some work has been done, all the more important because it was in areas which had hitherto been neglected. In Malaya the substantial progress already made was continued by competent British archaeologists like Sieveking at Gua Cha, and Williams-Hunt who discovered Greek sherds of the 4th century B.C. at Tengku Lembu (Perlis)[60]. In eastern Indochina E. Saurin continued his systematic study of the geological context and the chronology of the raised beaches of Annam; while many new sites were discovered in Laos, in western Cochinchina and in the Darlac area. In this last area, in the valley of the Srepok, G. Condominas found a lithophone which opens up new horizons and allows us to identify identical flakes which were already known but not understood.

We have seen that all along the foothills bordering the middle Mekong valley a line of "Moi forts" had been noted: each usually occupying the top of an isolated hill and consisting of a continuous circular earthwork surrounded by an external ditch. A first inventory of these works was published in 1957, but without investigation on the ground any theories about them were purely speculative[61]. After a survey from the air of the visible sites – clearly a tiny proportion of the whole – it seemed to me that they formed a complex of unusual importance, and in 1962 I excavated one of these camps at Mimot (Kompong Cham) *(Plates 1, 10)*, in the centre of the system, a structure with an external diameter of 200 metres. The excavation revealed a Neolithic stratum of astonishing richness, with fourteen levels and over 3 metres of deposits. This culture, provisionally called the Mimotian, is already represented by something like a thousand stone objects and more than twenty thousand sherds. As a result we have been able to reclassify other surface finds, defining a whole area in the centre of southern Indochina. The fort at Mimot has turned out to be one of the most important prehistoric sites in South-East Asia.

In Tonkin, P. I. Boriskovsky organised excavations from 1959 onwards which are clearly important, though we have still little information about them. It appears that some Mesolithic sites have been studied at Phu-to, near Mount Do (Thanh-hoa), and some Neolithic deposits found in the north-west of the country. The excavations have been particularly fruitful at Thien-duong (Thanh-hoa), where a cemetery of the Bronze Age has yielded material which is quite new, completely coherent, and dated by association with Chinese objects.

It is Siam, however, that has made the most spectacular entry on the stage of prehistory. In 1956 K. G. Heider drew attention to a considerable number of sites; but some information about them had already been gathered, in dramatic circumstances, by the Dutch prehistorian H. G. van Heekeren. As a Japanese prisoner of war he had worked on the notorious railway between Siam and Burma which ran up the valley of the Kwae Yai and crossed it on the famous bridge[62]; but in spite of the circumstances of the time he had realised the wealth of prehistoric remains which the valley contained. In 1961 a Danish and Thai expedition was organised under the leadership of Per Sorensen, who very appropriately invited van Heekeren to join the party. All along the course of the river, and in particular at Ban Kao and in the cave of Ong Ba, they discovered Bronze Age remains, including several drums, and a large Neolithic settlement, with burials which contained pottery of great beauty. The first reports stress the affinity of the material with the Gua Cha culture, and beyond it with Sa-huynh and – still farther away – Lung Shan in China. Later investigations have been extended to cover the whole of Siam, and each season has brought new material – including, for example, a cemetery near Lop'buri belonging to the end of the Neolithic and a huge Neolithic kitchen midden under the Khmer town of P'imai[63].

It is too early to offer any useful interpretation of this material, most of which has not even been published. But we know enough already to cast doubt on some of the working hypotheses which have hitherto been accepted. At the Neolithic level – which must now very probably be brought lower down in date – it is becoming more and more difficult to explain the observed facts solely by movements of population. Thus in the Mimotian the adze of trapezoidal and later of rectangular section follows the tanged adze of lenticular section without any gap, and is in turn superseded by the shouldered adze. There is no evidence to suggest that these changes were the result of "successive waves of Indonesians", and the last change at least seems to be connected with the spread of metal forms. It is true that scholars are increasingly – and, in our opinion, rightly – looking towards the great Chinese civilisations of Yang Shao and Lung Shan as the initial

115 →

113   114

sources of the Indochinese Neolithic culture (or, it may be, cultures). But this does not mean that we must explain the spread of these cultures solely by a series of migrations, which we must remember is only one among a number of possible hypotheses; still less that the new facts should be forced into conformity with the old theories. Thus the affinities of the material from the Kwae Yai valley with the Lung Shan culture are evident; but since it was believed that the spread must have taken place by sea it was necessary to invent a movement from east to west across the South China Sea in order to reconcile the theory, now hardened into an article of faith, with the new facts. The supporters of this theory would do well to remind themselves that a spread by land is at least equally possible.

As for the Dongsonian, here too more questions have been raised than have been answered. Criticism has been directed against the old theories – Goloubew's no less than Karlgren's – which certainly lack an archaeological basis; and some doubt has even been cast on the Chinese origins of the Dongsonian. It must be admitted that these objections are well founded[64]. But on the one hand no one has suggested any alternative to ethnographical comparisons as a means of explaining the subjects of the scenes represented in Dongsonian art; and on the other the stylistic connections with the bronzes of the Warring States, though less convincing than used to be thought, are still of significance. The latest archaeological discoveries in China, indeed, have considerably strengthened them. The most important in this respect are the discoveries at Shih Chai Shan, in the south of Yunnan-fu. In 1952–1953 and 1956–1957 more than twenty tombs dated to about 109 B.C. were excavated here. The valuable material discovered included some fifteen drums filled with cowries; one of them had on the top a scene made up of a hundred tiny bronze figures. They seem to be offering a human victim to some kind of dragon, and some of them are beating bronze drums hanging under a sloping roof. These finds confirmed a considerable body of investigations carried out in the area between Szechuan and Hongkong, which have made it possible to define a civilisation corresponding to that of Nan Yue. This benefited from the experience of the people of the Hwang-Ho, and flourished for several centuries before being swallowed up by them. It is difficult to avoid the conclusion that this culture was the source of the Dongsonian – unless it was itself derived from the Dongsonian. And certainly we must note the existence at the same period of a southern Dongsonian in Cambodia, Malaya, Siam and Indonesia, which was clearly an important province and may have developed more or less independently *(Plates 5, 6, 7)*.

Let us, therefore, conclude cautiously that it is necessary to review the whole problem and establish the chronology and the relationship of the different bodies of evidence. It may nevertheless be suggested that the supposed Thraco-Cimmerian origins are becoming increasingly problematic, and that in any event there is no basis for the recent theories which went so far as to recognise "Hellenistic" influences in the funerary ritual of Dong-son[65]. In reality the presence of objects from the Mediterranean on the shores of Indochina, which was at the origin of these theories, is very easily explained by contacts made by sea, and more specifically by the formation of the first Indianised civilisations in Indochina. After all, the prehistory of the peninsula is still in its infancy. Great things can be expected of it, but in the meantime caution is called for. We can see this at once by looking at the map: throughout this whole area, as large as western Europe, only ten or twelve sites, clustered together in four groups some hundred of miles apart, have so far been properly described. If we think of the great body of research that has been necessary to establish a proper picture of the European Neolithic alone we can judge how much still remains to be done in Indochina.

The Formation of the Civilisations of Indochina

Much ink has flowed in the argument between those who believed in the decisive and almost exclusive influence of India – or China – in creating the specific character of Indochinese civilisation and those who supported, sometimes with great vehemence, the so-called "local genius". It must be confessed that the former had an unfair advantage in their command of the considerable body of knowledge already built up in their fields. Often the great Indianists or Sinologists thought of Indochina as a distraction from more important matters, a field in which they gave an occasional helping hand to fellow scholars who had trouble in reading their texts or, worse still, had no texts to read. In dealing with a building which corresponded exactly with the Indian norms, for example, they would as a rule interpret it in accordance with these norms, and would then conclude that these were all-important and had been taken over in their entirety by the natives. But they sometimes lacked a sense of evolution, and they also forgot that a system of formal rules may lend itself to more than one interpretation. Because the mediaeval church drew its techniques and the essential features of its iconography from Roman art, or because Christianity is of Jewish origin, no one has thought to conclude that a cathedral was Roman or Jewish. And roughly the same period of time elapsed between the arrival of the Indians and the building of the great sanctuaries of Angkor. Moreover we have no idea of the function or the exact meaning which the Khmers, for example, attributed at a given period to forms which had been in use for so long; we do not even know if they still spoke Sanskrit.

In any event there are many aspects of Indian and Chinese archaeology which require further study. The chronology of the Gupta and Pallava styles, which left such a mark on Indochina, is not nearly exact enough, and there has been no systematic study of the Indian objects discovered in South-East Asia[66]. The Chinese monuments are well known; but there is no doubt that an archaeological study of Yun-nan or the Canton area during the Han dynasty, for example, would throw light on the formation of Tonkin[67]. And, more generally, insufficient attention has been paid to the effects of the political history of India and China on the development of Indochina[68].

The defenders of the originality of the native culture, for their part, have suffered a series of setbacks which were no more than they deserved for the inadequacy of their methods. Knowing that no text will ever tell us anything about the modes of thought of the protohistorical civilisations of Indochina, they might at least have studied them archaeologically and thus established the nature of their material cultures. After all, we cannot measure an electrical current unless we have taken a reading of the two contacts and noted the result of the discharge; and in this case we know only the source, we know nothing of the receiving end, and not even very much about the consequences. When some progress has been made in this direction the controversies will die down of themselves, for their sterility will have become evident to all.

Fortunately the trend in this direction has already begun. The discoveries in western Cochinchina which enabled Fu-nan to be identified have already been mentioned[69]. From 1951 onwards the author carried out a complete air survey of this area which revealed hundreds of canals and some dozens of cities, and has made it possible to recognise and classify the types, and thus pave the way for excavation. Although, so far, no work has been done on the ground, at least we know where to look. In southern Siam, particularly round Nak'on Pathom, many cities surrounded by earthworks have been identified on the ground and from the air[70]. It is not known whether they are to be associated with Fu-nan or, more probably, with the early period of Dvaravati – though it may be that the two cannot be distinguished. We can get some idea of the development of this Mon civilisation from the stucco work found at Ku Bua in 1961 by the Thai Archaeological Survey. At the other end of the country we need to study the origins of Haripunjaya – probably connected with south-western Thina, where an individual style of Buddhist art developed very early. In the valley of the Se Mun and as far away as the Mekong many towns have been identified, almost circular in shape, surrounded by earthworks and served by a system of water supply[71]. They seem likely to be cities of Tchen-la, and offer an exciting field for excavation. In Burma U Aung Thaw has been working at Peikthanomyo since 1959, excavating tumuli containing cinerary urns and a city which apparently belongs to the end of the Mon period and shows very few Indian remains[72]. Recent researches at Prome, which have for the first time revealed traces of native settlement, are no less promising.

Systematic excavation in the Malay peninsula ought to be at least as rewarding. A critical study of the Chinese pottery, which is the basis of Quaritch Wales's chronology, shows that not a single fragment is earlier than the 9th century[73]. The investigations by Alastair Lamb in connection with the reconstruction of the temple on the Sungei Batu Pahat have not taken us much farther back, and it looks as if these architectural remains are more probably to be associated with the large islands of the south. Lamb has also discovered a number of sites astonishingly rich in Chinese pottery, particularly on the island of Ko Kao, near Ta Kua Po, and at Pengkalan Bujang in the estuary of the Merbok. From a first examination it appears that the material ranges in date from the Southern Sung to the Ming period, and this agrees with observations at Angkor on these same exports. Thus there still remains a considerable hiatus between the Indian expansion which is attested in Malaya by objects of the 4th–5th centuries and the earliest known archaeological sites. But there is no reason why a connection should not be found, and in this field alone there is enough work to keep the archaeologists busy for decades. And in Champa and Vietnam too we have seen that the sites are also known: here too there is a great future for field archaeology.

Monumental Archaeology

Although we are ignorant of their exact origin it might be supposed that we know a good deal about the great buildings of Indochina, since they are dated and can be fitted into a well established scheme of stylistic analysis. This is true if we think back to the time of their discovery, when there might be a margin of error of several centuries in their dating or identification. It is true also if we compare the progress achieved in Cambodia with the uncertainty about some of the largest sanctuaries in Indonesia, or even in Champa or Burma. But if we look more closely at the material discussed in these studies, we are dismayed to find how rough and ready they actually are. Inventories which are described, in all good faith, as "exhaustive"[74], are riddled with errors: a monument may be given one storey too many or too few, a roof may be described as cradle-shaped instead of in the lotus-bud shape, merely because this is thought to be more appropriate to the style of the supposed architect. Apart from the records of Vietnamese monuments published by L. Bezacier, there are no monographs containing the analysis, the plans and the illustrations necessary to give a complete or even an adequate idea of any of the monuments of Indochina. To take one example, the Bayon *(Plates 118, 119, 130)* – one of the most famous, the most important and the most fascinating temples of Angkor – is known from a plan and an architectural analysis which are accepted as accurate because we owe them to "the penetrating eye of an architect"[75]. In fact, however, the plan was obtained by a survey of a quarter of the building, which was then turned round to produce the whole; but by an ironic mischance the part surveyed contained an extra tower, and this was then repeated in the other parts which in fact contained no such tower. The rest of the plan is no less inaccurate, even omitting the whole of one half-gallery. When the temple was built, apart from additions which are not the same as those described, several towers were modified or had only three, or even two sculptured surfaces. None of these facts is correctly analysed or recorded. And yet for the last forty years there has been endless discussion and interpretation of the symbolism of the Bayon, which depends entirely on such things as the exact layout, and the number of towers, and the number of faces carved on it.

In any event our knowledge of most of the temples is confined to the parts now visible and to a few internal features, like the axial wells, discovered by Trouvé at Angkor. There has been no stratigraphical investigation of the foundations, of the site, or of its earlier use. Some of the temples at Angkor *(Plates 120, 121, 122, 123, 124, 125, 126, 127, 128)* had been known for sixty years, "excavated" after a fashion, and frequently discussed in the literature; but when at last they were properly studied they were found to be raised on large understructures, to be surrounded by walls, ancillary buildings and entrance pavilions, and to be built on top of earlier settlements – none of which had hitherto been suspected. In this field only the complete reconstruction of a building allows us to understand it completely; and we know that this is also the only way to save buildings[76]. This, therefore, is the aim which lies before us, for we have a responsibility for the preservation of the buildings in our care.

If we consider the archaeology of smaller finds there is even less to show. Apart from two recent studies written from the point of view of the collector, and the typological description of the material from Oc-eo, we cannot point to as many as twenty printed pages on the pottery of these areas, its stratigraphy and its spread – although, as we shall see[77], pottery probably offers the key to many of our problems. And much the same could be said about many other gaps in our knowledge.

The History of Art

This is the best written chapter – a chapter sometimes, indeed, brilliantly written – in the archaeological history of Indochina. The details still, however, need to be filled out; for example in Burma, as the reader may have gathered from the difficulty I had writing the few lines about Burma in an earlier chapter. All we can do is to follow the genealogy of the temples through several reigns; we have no real understanding of the characteristics or development of the various styles.

Other fields have not been explored at all, except perhaps from the iconographic point of view. There has been no study of painting in Burma; fortunately we are now better off in Siam, where the Archaeological Survey has undertaken systematic recording and Miss E. Lyons has applied her gifts to the task. Only the history of art – or archaeological excavation – could give an idea of the later periods, for example of post-Angkorian Cambodia *(Plates 111, 132-134)*; and the results would be valuable, for there is statuary and painting of the greatest interest.[78] And even after the arrival of the Westerners there is a fascinating chapter to be written about the influence of their art on the various countries, from Thai painting with its representations of the "long-nosed barbarians" and its vista'd landscapes to the Louis XV *décor* of the Cambodian pagodas.

It is important, however, to give an accurate description of the examples chosen for study and to establish their relevance. Earlier writers, reasonably enough, used specimens which were readily accessible in museums. It could easily be demonstrated that many of our currently accepted ideas flow from the simple physical fact that their authors have persisted endlessly in photographing one particular statue rather than another. And are we even sure that the photograph is a correct representation? The camera lens sees things differently from the human eye; it sees only part of them, and may give a false impression if the wrong angle has been chosen or the picture is distorted by the lighting. It is easy to forget how techniques of graphic reproduction, even the most advanced, can alter the appearance of an object; and this applies also to plans. Nor are the methods of our museums sufficiently developed to allow us to put implicit faith in their material. We remember, for example, that a statue, frequently illustrated, has recently received its arms and other attributes which had been lying neglected a few yards away in the same museum. And too much importance has sometimes

117

118

← 119, 120, 121, 122, 123, 124, 125, 126, 127, 128

129

130

been attributed to the most striking specimens, without considering whether this in itself did not make them exceptional.

There is not so much material that an exhaustive, or nearly exhaustive, count is out of the question; and only a statistical approach is able, even in part, to fill the gaps which result from the ravages of time and the accidents of discovery. A striking example is given by the Khmer bronzes. Having just completed a list of them, I find that more than two thirds are Buddhist pieces in the style of Jayavarman VII *(Plates 138-143)*. Must we conclude that the style developed in this king's reign or for the purposes of Buddhism? There is a great deal of reliable evidence, however, that the style was in favour, and perhaps to an even greater extent, at an earlier period. The more probable explanation is that since metal was scarce it was the practice to throw older pieces periodically into the melting pot, either to renew them or out of zeal for the new religion. But only a solid statistical basis could provide supporting evidence. Similarly there has not yet been sufficient study of the technique of the artist-carvers *(Plates 132-133)*. And yet on Khmer monuments which were never finished we find work at all stages of completion, illustrating the methods of the carvers and explaining certain conventions *(Plate 30)*. The need now is to go beyond casual sampling and undertake an exhaustive study. That this can be done has been demonstrated in a masterly way by Dupont's work on pre-Angkorian statuary and Griswold's on a particular school of Thai statuary.

Naturally enough the first studies were directed towards the large buildings founded by the kings, the only ones which as a rule were mentioned in the texts, and more humble monuments were neglected. Here again the statistical basis of our studies must be extended, and in this way we may hope on the one hand to be able to define the characteristics of the different styles more closely, and on the other to distinguish personal styles and secondary or local schools which may be of the greatest interest. This type of investigation is easy to carry out, and the Thai Archaeological Survey is achieving very satisfactory results in this direction in the north-east of the country. Some progress has also been made in Cambodia. At the same time it is important to analyse the buildings with the greatest care. One of Philippe Stern's achievements has been to establish that the monuments of Jaya-varman's reign had been several times altered and enlarged. Each new excavation at Angkor shows that this is true of all the Khmer temples, and it seems also to be true of the sanctuaries of Burma – more particularly because it was always a pious tradition to decorate them, enlarge them, or at least regild them. Only a rigorous analysis of this kind can enable us to be sure that we are not taking the part for the whole or – still worse – apply-ing to the whole building a date recorded on a later addition or a stele originally erected elsewhere. Such a date can never be more than a *terminus a quo*. This could easily be demonstrated for Koh Ker, for example, or for the whole chronology of Khmer art from Yasovarman to Rajendra-varman, which is in need of detailed revision *(Plates 32, 45)*.

Nomenclature, Periods and Categories

One essential problem is the chronological and typological classification of the facts. The first objective was, inevitably, to establish local lines of descent; but at the end of the day what real value have these, apart from their convenience? We cannot be sure that our categories always correspond to reality. To take an example from Khmer art, we cannot really be content to distinguish only one style, that of Banteay Srei, between the Koh Ker and Khleang styles, and to classify Pre Rup merely as a transitional stage. The classification of the styles of Thai art is unsatisfactory, and the styles of Burmese art have not even been defined. The terminology we use is of particular importance since it inevitably creates the concepts which condition our thinking. The practice of naming a style after a characteristic building can be justified; but would it not be better to use the name of the king who built it, which has at least the advantage of defining a moment in history and in the development of social habits and techniques? On a smaller scale, it must be admitted that we have not yet found a satisfactory way of dividing the history of Indochina into periods presenting certain common characteristics; nor, for that matter, are we in a position to measure the rhythms of history, to judge why at one time or place there was stagnation, at another a sudden spurt ahead.

Most of these problems are a matter for comparative studies or for large "horizontal" studies in particular fields; and over the greater part of the field these have not even been begun. Indochinese archaeology has suffered from a division into separate compartments as a result of the small number of workers in this field, political separatism, the high degree of specialisation which was unavoidable, and the complexity of the facts. A new impetus was given to Khmer studies by the discoveries made in Indonesia and the methods developed there[79]; and Khmer studies in turn guided and helped research in Siam and Champa. Philippe Stern was able to perceive the Javanese influences in Khmer and Cham art; but other influences, like the connections between Burma and the rest of Indochina or the adoption of some Cham themes by Vietnam, are little understood. Looking farther afield, we have still to establish the great currents of history which affected the whole of Indochina, China, and India – as has already been briefly noted, for example, for the 13th century. Conversely, there has been insufficient appreciation of the crucial part Indochina must have played at the beginning of history as a bridgehead of Asia towards the Pacific. From Indochina, or through Indochina, came the great movements of peoples or cultures which then reached out as far as Hawaii and perhaps even to the coasts of America. Finally "horizontal" studies of particular fields of Indochinese archaeology – for example Buddhist architecture or the techniques of the organisation of space, to mention only two – are among the most promising lines of future advance.

The Role of Archaeology

Were it not for the title of this series, we should have been tempted to suggest as our conclusion that the archaeology of Indochina does not yet exist, except perhaps in the field of prehistory. Let us be clear what we mean by archaeology. It is used here in the sense of the study of the material remains of a civilisation. When these remains are buildings they belong, of course, in large part to the history of art, a study which is already solidly established. Similarly for epigraphy. But in general the immense resources of our discipline have so far barely been tapped – scarcely even suspected.

Almost until the 1950s no excavation worthy of the name had been carried out in Indochina on any historical site. This was one of the consequences of an isolation which in this field was complacently accepted. It is no use pleading that excavation methods are of recent development. With the aid of a little care and thought, Kidder in the United States, Pitt Rivers in Britain and Flinders Petrie in Egypt had discovered stratigraphy long before 1914. But Indochina had not the advantage of excavations by foreign archaeologists and the competition and emulation to which they give rise. Except in the field of philology these studies were all too often left in the hands of the technicians, who were sometimes able – as in the case of G. Trouvé – to discover the methods for themselves, but in general do not seem to have become masters of their subject. It is hardly surprising when we see one of them, dignified with the title of "Inspector of the Archaeological Service", exclaiming, when initiated by the great prehistorian van Stein-Callenfels into rigorous excavation methods: "The only disadvantage of this method... is the length of time involved – sometimes several years for the excavation of a few cubic yards of ground"[80]. The aim is not, however, to lay waste acres of ground or dig up statues by the ton. Admittedly the complexity of the problems and their urgency made it necessary to proceed with care: it was not possible to do everything, and certain excavations were not an immediate necessity. But if most of the studies of buildings, for example, had been conscientiously executed we should have had more to show for the work that has been done.

Some Guiding Threads

As a result, the idea of the barrenness of Indochina in this field has become firmly entrenched. And yet a few excavations at Angkor have recently doubled the number of Khmer bronzes found there in the previous fifty years *(Plates 139-145)*, and multiplied the pottery a hundredfold; and this pottery provides a chronological thread of absolute reliability which is found everywhere from the earliest period. Similarly with the pottery of Sawank'alok and Thanh-hoa. Better still is the evidence provided by the pottery which was exported from China in tens of thousands of pieces, particularly from the 10th century onwards; these can be exactly dated and identified by the regular development of shapes and materials, and they are found throughout Indochina and Indonesia, in India, Africa, Madagascar and the Middle East. Like the Proto-Corinthian pottery and the *terra sigillata* of the Mediterranean, this pottery enables us to date sites of all kinds, and to follow throughout Asia the pattern of a far-flung movement of trade.

There are new techniques, too, recently added to our armoury and crying out to be used. First there are the new methods of absolute dating. The first carbon 14 datings are awaited for the prehistoric sites of Siam, and trials have also been made on some Thai and Khmer statues in wood. The study of pollens, which are found in great quantity and in excellent preservation in the soils of Indochina, reveals the development and cultivation of useful plants by man. Thus rice, for example – its origins, its cultivation and its spread – is fundamental to any study of the growth of human settlement in Indochina. Soon we ought to have palaeo-botanic maps of the Angkor area showing, century by century, what was cultivated there.

Aerial archaeology has revealed the planning of the cities, with their roads, their irrigation works, the division and use of the land *(Plates 127, 135, 136)*. Estimates have been made of the evaporation of water stored up in the irrigation system. Stratigraphical sections of the canals of Angkor show the process of silting up year by year in the form of thin alternate layers of sand and mud, which reflect each rainy season, each period of spate and of drought *(Plate 137)*. And all this reveals to us the very basis of the life of the people of Angkor. Without this evidence we could not follow the course of their development, their success and their failure; and, at a higher level, we could not understand their social organisation, or the temples they built as the supreme expression of this organisation, if we were unable to reconstruct their economic, social and technical history. It is not a question of subordinating the former to the latter: on the contrary, we shall often find the demands of religion leading to solutions which, technically, were aberrant. But we must include both aspects if we want to have the whole picture.

To this total historical picture archaeology can make its contribution. It cannot, of course, do this by itself, except perhaps in the prehistoric period[81]. It is well aware of its limitations. Nothing can replace a written text for telling us what men thought, or even for informing us about their law, their system of values, or their techniques. But there is a place too for the archaeologist who, competently and in all modesty, sets about his task of gathering the material evidence, describing it, counting it, classifying it, dating it, and seeking so far as possible to build it up into a general picture, which is often remarkable in its completeness.

Sylvian Lévi remarked that "a man who cannot be a philologist becomes an archaeologist; if he cannot be an archaeologist he becomes a prehistorian;

and if he cannot be a prehistorian he becomes an ethnologist". Are we to take this sally literally? There is some truth, at least, in this statement of the order of merit of which students in these disciplines are sometimes aware, even though unconsciously, in their relationships with each other. The statement also expresses a reality – the respective importance of the sources. For after all, when there are no texts[82], we must do our best with the remains of buildings, or if need be with carved stones or with habits handed down from generation to generation.

This summing up, this statement of credits and sometimes of debits, is not conceived solely with the idea of denying the achievement of our predecessors. That would be a foolish thing to do, for we shall soon find ourselves, in our turn, outdated and exposed to fierce attack by a new and better equipped generation. Our only concern has been – as it surely ought to be – to take stock of our exact position, to be ready at any time to reconsider the results already achieved, and to keep abreast of the movement of ideas and the results attained in parallel fields, so that in due time we can hand on to our successors an improved discipline which can look forward to fresh achievements.

143, 144, 145 →

141

142

CONCLUSION

VII

Reflections on Indochina

It is fashionable to cast doubt on the validity of the historical sciences, on the ground that basically they are no more than the projection of an individual curiosity. Archaeologists are not only "a handful of antiquaries who take a macabre delight in removing the wrappings from dead gods"[83]. So long as they overcome the temptations of dogmatism and concern themselves with establishing the conditions which determine the validity and the limits of their observations, so long as they accept that no researches, however thorough, can ever guarantee that they have exhausted the existing documents, and that the material they use represents only a residue which cannot be measured, either for quantity or quality, against what has been lost: if they accept all this, then they can organise their facts and seek to interpret them. When one thinks that Philippe Stern proposed a probable dating of the monuments of the reign of Jayavarman VII, and that ten years later a series of inscriptions was discovered giving exactly the dates suggested, it is evident that the art historian has justified himself. When in an excavation at Angkor we conclude from a convergent series of internal indications that a particular level belongs to the 12th century; when this level, and this level alone, yields Chinese pottery dated by independent researchers to the same period on the basis of written texts and their knowledge of the potters; and when finally the same objects appear on an Indonesian site where they are again limited to the 12th century by local inscriptions: then we may legitimately regard the fact as established, and may go on – subject to confirmation – to assign the same date to a burial in Madagascar which has yielded identical vases and cannot be dated in any other way.

Where, however, our knowledge is based only on the recurrence of certain data we are not entitled to give it the authority of a "science", to formulate rules, still less to extrapolate these rules in space or time. We may conclude with H. I. Marrou that "the validity of the concepts used by the historian is – we must not say relative – dependent, rather, not so much on the personality of the historian, or on his mentality, or on the time at which he is writing, as on the truth, on the philosophy – implicit and preferably implicit – which has allowed him to develop them"[84]. The ultimate question we must ask ourselves, therefore, is what are the reasons for our investigations and what result they may be expected to achieve. Even though we can hardly claim to do more than give our personal reply, we must nevertheless venture to do so, for this is, after all, our fundamental problem.

The basis of our concern with archaeology or, more generally, with Oriental studies is, quite simply, a curiosity about man. This proposition may not be generally accepted, and plenty of others have been suggested. The Orient and its "mysteries" have appeared to many as the source of a new religion; and, to speak plainly, the mystagogues and the theosophists have done great harm to a field of study which had already enough trouble in organising itself. True, they themselves vehemently condemn "official science" and deny its right to interpret sublime truths; but after all they are free to do better if they can. And though there may be mysteries hidden in the stones of Angkor they must allow us at least to count the stones: surely this is a necessary prerequisite of any further study? At the other end of the spectrum – or rather of the halo which surrounds these studies – archaeology is regarded as a synonym for treasure hunt; the archaeologist is a man who after long pondering deciphers some magic formula, hurries off to the desert, digs a hole in the sand, and finally lays bare a mummy of solid gold. At this stage there seem to be two possibilities: either the archaeologist dies, a victim of the Pharaoh's curse, or he becomes a member of the Institut de France – and it is not clear which of these alternatives, both equally fatal, is worse. It might be interesting to study the causes of these fantasies. A desire to escape from the confined atmosphere of our own civilisation? The influence of powerful vested interests – the mass media, the dealers in antiquities, the travel agencies? Or merely an uninformed but perfectly laudable interest in the exotic? It is, of course, only one aspect of the "explorer complex" so lucidly analysed by Claude Lévi-Strauss[85]. We must note with regret that it is impossible, faced with new facts, merely to record them, without experiencing either disgust or passion. And just because the exotic offers us the heady opportunity to judge other peoples it is all the less likely to arouse the desire to know more about them[86].

Even where they have achieved their most substantial results Oriental studies have not yet become an integral part of our culture – though this would surely be their final justification. If we open the *Petit Larousse* we find that the article on Cambodia is illustrated by a piece of Cham sculpture, and we are told that Burma "was part of the Indian Empire until 1947" – the only reference thought necessary to two thousand years of history[87]. It would be even more depressing to survey the comprehensive works on world history and archaeology which are so popular nowadays – and are supposed to be written by experts – or to read the syllabuses of our universities. We must of course accept that there is a considerable time lag between the moment when a theory is accepted as reasonable by the professionals and the time when it becomes part of the general body of knowledge[88]. The disciplines with which we are concerned are very young, and are still in course of development; thus there are still differences of opinion among their practitioners, and this naturally inspires a certain amount of scepticism. And finally the essential knowledge does not reside in the producer of learned works using in his study material which he knows only at second hand, but in the practical scholar who is able to repeat – or at least to follow critically – the process of reasoning that led to a certain conclusion, and is prepared to reconsider this conclusion at once if there is any modification of its premises. We can admit all this, but it is nevertheless true that some parts of the field are already established and might well take their place in the picture we have of the world. That this has not happened is due, I fear, to the distaste still felt by many intelligent people for anything that cannot, directly or indirectly, claim a Greek ancestry. And thus, paradoxically, they deprive themselves of one of the most exciting rewards of that intellectual tradition of enlightened curiosity which has been such a characteristically Greek quality from the time of Herodotus onwards.

Moreover we must always bear in mind that these systematic studies of Asia are the work of Europeans, and thus reflect specifically European modes of thought. This does not necessarily make them the best, and they are certainly not the only, studies. China, for example, has throughout its history, through its conquests, its travellers and its trade, gradually elaborated its own conception of South-East Asia, to which it gave the specific name of K'un-lun. The Chinese even undertook systematic voyages of exploration, as for example under the early Ming emperors with the squadrons of the eunuch Cheng Ho. And just as we are trying to do, they fitted their picture of the area into their own particular scheme of things. They interpreted the facts, of course, according to their own system of values. For example Chou Ta-kuan, the traveller who visited Angkor at the end of the 13th century, ended his description of the court with an expression both of his admiration and of his sense of superiority as a Chinese: "We thus see that these people, although barbarians, are not without knowledge of what is due to a prince"[89]. If this feeling of superiority disconcerts us, let us think of our own. After all, the Chinese historians were no less competent than our own; and where should we be without them? This is not the only example we could give. At the beginning of the 16th century, for example, when the Tokugawa *shoguns* encouraged commercial exchanges, a pilgrim named Shimano Kenryo visited Cambodia, though under the impression that he was in Gandhara, in the sacred places of Buddhism. He described Angkor Vat, and even drew a plan of it which has been preserved, and which constitutes the first archaeological study of the temple. Each of the civilisations of Indochina, too, has its personal vision of its own past; and this is a valuable source of information which we must not neglect. We must be clear that when we say that Mouhot discovered Angkor we mean only that he revealed it to Europe. For centuries the Cambodians had been living near the temple and were familiar with it, so that – subconsciously, perhaps, but none the less effectively – it formed part of their intellectual background. It is not without significance that King Ang Duong, in the period before the protectorate, chose the silhouette of the great shrine as the symbol on his coins and his flag. There are many Cambodian legends about Angkor, which are something more than tales purporting to record historical events: perhaps one day they will be shown to be myths, the norms of a society perpetuated in the folk memory.

These links with the past are further strengthened by religion. In Burma and Thailand the restoration of ancient Buddhist monuments is still a meritorious work – though one which, paradoxically, is sometimes to the disadvantage of archaeology. Similarly the possession of a statue or other object which had been charged with meaning for its previous owners – often the vanquished – has always played a part in what might be called sentimental archaeology. After his conquest of Arakan in 1785 King Bodawpaya caused an immense statue of Buddha to be dismantled and sawn into pieces, and then transported it to his capital – an enterprise which employed 12,000 men – and set it up in the Arakan pagoda. And there, also, he collected more than six hundred ancient inscriptions – no doubt in order to confirm the title of the monasteries to the land, but also, perhaps, to maintain a link with the traditions of the past. Much of the material in the museums at Bangkok and Phnom Penh comes from the collections of the royal families; and these collections cannot be the result solely of hoarding or religious feeling, for many of the objects have no intrinsic value or are associated with Hinduism, which had long been rejected.

It is true, however, that Western travellers found most of the remains in ruins, and so little understood that the local inhabitants often believed that only gods could have built them. It is a picture that has perhaps been a little too popular, giving rise to some well-known passages about "the striking and painful contrast with the lamentable state of barbarism which afflicts the surviving descendants of the great people that built these monuments"[90]. What orientalist has never yielded, unconsciously it may be, to this feeling of satisfaction with what has been achieved? The story of Europe's artistic heritage is one long sordid tale of negligence and destruction, for motives that were either squalid or pointless, and the sudden change of heart displayed by our own century is probably no more than a sign of bad conscience and of our inability to believe that we can better do than our ancestors; nor is it so consistent that we can always be sure of the result.

It is nevertheless true that the basis of our knowledge about the past of Indochina, for example, has been put together and is still being developed by Western scholars. What is more serious is that they have not always done all they might to train in their methods the successors who must be found locally. There is a real difficulty here. The heritage of part of the human race has, for all practical purposes, been appropriated by an alien system which is sufficiently powerful and sufficiently rich to afford a kind of intellectual raree-show. And it is humiliating for those who are, after all, the rightful heirs to this inheritance to have to depend on charity. We have been reminded of this often enough[91]. And we must admit that this attitude *has* existed. Take Raffles, writing with the naive enthusiasm of the period: "(We must) collect the scattered remains of the literature of these countries... The rays of intellect now divided and lost will be concentrated into a focus from which they will be radiated with an added lustre, brightened and strengthened by our superior lights... If the time shall come when (Britain's) Empire shall have passed away, these monuments of her virtue will endure, when her triumphs shall have become an empty name... Let (Britain) be remembered... as the gale of spring, reviving the slumbering seeds of mind, and calling them to life from the winter of ignorance"[92]. And a century later another writer, no less sincere, was to say: "A European nation which takes possession of an ancient and historic land is in a sense accountable to the civilised world for the memories entrusted to its care;

it has a duty to preserve them and make them known. It is a debt of honour which a nation cannot repudiate without losing the respect of others and its own self-respect"[93].

It would be no less unjust to deny what has been accomplished, or to belittle the motives of those who accomplished it. They had a sense of mission but they also had the sincere and disinterested enthusiasm of civilised men: "Though they still stand after ten centuries, (the monuments of Angkor) are threatened by the ravages of time, weather and vegetation. Steps to preserve them are urgently necessary. Local resources are insufficient to meet the full cost of what must be done: we must look also for private help... It must not be said that Angkor suffered more from indifference... than from the ravages of time"[94]. Like every human enterprise, this one has had its lights and shadows. To understand both the lights and the shadows is the best preparation for the task which we must pursue together.

SYNOPTIC
CHRONOLOGICAL TABLE

		INDIA	BURMA	MALAYA	SIAM
400	900	**Chola**	**PAGAN**	SRIVIJAYA	DVARAVATI
300			*Zokthok* *Bupaya*		**Haripunjaya**
200			*Petleik*		
		Rajaraja	*Chola raids*		
100	1000	Mahmud of Ghazni		Airlangga	*Khmer dominance* *Panom Fan*
0			Anoratha *Shwezigon*		*P'imai*
100			*Shwesando* *Pithakathaik* *Lokananda* Kyanzittha	*Khmer dominance*	
200	1100	Vikramaditya	*Ananda* Alaungsithu	Ch'aiya	**Lamp'un**
		Sena **Hoysala**	*Thatbynnyu*	Ligor	Aditaraja
300			Narathu *Dhammayangyi*		Lopburi **Sukhot'ai**
400			*Mimalaung Gyaung*		Jayavarman VII
	1200	Mahmud of Ghor	Narapatisithu *Dhammayanzika*		*Wat Kukut*
500		*Mamluks*	*Htilominlo* *Mangalacetiya* *Kondawgyi*	*End of Khmer dominance*	
			Narathihapate		
600			*Mongol attacks*	*End of Srivijaya*	*Thai princedoms*
	1300	*Moslems of Deccan*		*Thai at Ligor*	*Chieng Mar*
			Kyozwo	Grahi	Rama Kamheng
700		Firoz Shah	**Taungu** **Ava**		**Lavo** **U Tong** **Ayuthya**
		Timur			Ramesuen
	1400				
800					**Lamp'un**
			Shwedagon	*Moslem emirates*	Chieng Mai
	1500				Tiloka
900		*Portuguese*		*Portuguese at Malacca*	*Ch'aiya*

CAMBODIA		CHAMPA	VIETNAM	CHINA
EMPIRE OF ANGKOR				**Five Dynasties**
		Khuong-my	*Ngo*	
		Mi-son A 1	*Nai la*	
Jayavarman IV	*Koh Ker*			
Rajendravarman	*Pre Rup*		*Co-loa*	**Later Han**
	Banteay Srei	Harivarman II	Thien-khe	
				Northern **Sung**
Jayavarman V	*Khleang*			*Hsi-Hsia*
	Phimeanakas		Earlier **Le**	
Suryavarman I	*Ta Keo*	**Vijaya**	**Ly**	
			Ha-noi	
Udayitya II	*Baphuon*	*Annamite attacks*	DAI-VIET	
			Ly Thanh-ton	
Cham attacks		Harivarman IV	*Phat-tich*	
		Chan-lo		
Harshavarman III		*Po Nagar*	*Binh-son*	
Jayavarman VI	*Vat Phu*	**Binh-dinh**	Ly Nhon-ton	
Suryavarman II	*Angkor Vat*		*Long-doi-son*	
	B. Samre			Southern **Sung**
	Preah Pithu	*Khmer conquest*	*Thien-phuc*	
Dharanindra-	*Beng Mealea*			*Jurchids*
varman	*Preah Khan*		Ly Thanh-ton	
Cham attacks				
	Ta Prohm	Jaya Indrav. IV	ANNAM	
	Preah Khan		Ly Cao-ton	
	Bayon	*Khmer conquest*		
	Terraces			Gengis Khan
		Hung-thanh		
		Liberation	**Iran**	
				Ogotai
Indravarman II		*Thap-mam*		**Yuan**
		Mongol attacks	*Mongol attacks*	Kublai
	Mangalartha	*Po Klaung Garai*		*Marco Polo*
Thai attacks		*Conquest of North by Vietnam*		
		Che Bong Nga	*Cham raids*	**Ming**
Capture of Angkor				
			Ho	
Fall of Angkor		*Vietnamese conquest*	*Ming conquest*	
CAMBODIA			**Le**	
Ang Chan			*Lam-son*	
Barom Reachea I			**Mac**	

NOTES

Abbreviations

B.E.F.E.O.: Bulletin de l'Ecole Française d'Extrême-Orient
B.S.E.I.: Bulletin de la Société des Etudes Indochinoises
E.F.E.O.: Ecole Française d'Extrême-Orient
I.D.E.O.: Imprimerie d'Extrême-Orient

[1] This book uses an extremely simple system of transcription, which approximately reproduces the present-day pronunciation if the vowels are given the same values as in Italian; an exception is made for names with a traditional English spelling. This seems the best method in a general work of this kind. The very number of different languages spoken in Indochina is of course also a problem, and the difficulty is increased by the divergence between spelling and pronunciation which is often found in languages like Cambodian or Burmese.

[2] For further study of the geography of Indochina, the following books are recommended: P. Gourou, *L'Asie*, Hachette, Paris, 1953, and C. A. Fisher, *South East Asia*, Methuen, London, 1964. See also H. H. Loofs, *Südost Asiens Fundamente*, Safari Vg, Berlin, 1964.

[3] For a fuller study of these problems, see: B. P. Groslier, "Milieu et Evolution en Asie", *B.S.E.I.*, XXVII, 3, 1952.

[4] Though it seemed necessary to give a summary of Indochinese history in this work, a detailed survey would have gone beyond the scope of the series. This can be found in G. Coedès, *The Making of South East Asia*, Routledge and Kegan Paul, London, 1966. This little book by a philologist of great authority gives a careful account, from this point of view, of the political history of the area. But for a study of archaeology and the history of art as an expression of society, I may be permitted to refer to my book on *Indochina* in the series "Art of the World" (Methuen, London, 1962). To some extent the present work is a counterpart, a critical reflection of this earlier *Indochina*, in which I purposely confined myself to setting out the classic themes. Since these two works contain the essential bibliography the present notes need give only references on particular points discussed, and to recent publications.

[5] There may also be a tendency to adjust a theory to fit in with linguistic classifications: see the surprising results of this in G. Coedès, *op. cit.*, pp. 26-31. The linguistic classifications adopted by Coedès are of course those generally accepted in the light of the latest research; but it is at least premature to make them coincide with a system of palaeontology which is still in process of development, and even more so to use this to explain them.

[6] These are purely arbitrary judgments based on the time allowed for the movements of peoples which are supposed to have constituted Indochina. We consider in chapter VI the validity of these latest hypotheses.

[7] It may be useful to give the Annamite versions of these Chinese terms, which are frequently encountered in the literature. Chinese Lo is Vietnamese Lac; Nan Yue is Nam Viet; and Chiao Chih is Giao-chi, which was deformed successively by European travellers into Cauchin, Cochin, and finally, by way of the French Cochin de Chine, became Cochinchina. I have retained terms like Annam and Tonkin which are accepted in modern usage and are legitimate when used in the geographical sense without any political implications.

[8] I am well aware how arbitrary is the term "Indochinese". I use it here simply to indicate that in my view the Vietnamese Chams and other peoples of the peninsula had probably not yet

achieved the individual identities which were later associated with these specific names. It would be a fascinating study to see how, as a result of adopting, or accepting, a particular culture, the various groups who occupied Indochina became Vietnamese, Chams, and so on.

[9] A recent important study of this problem is P. Wheatley, *The Golden Khersonese*, University of Malaya Press, London, 1961.

[10] Nor – lacking texts in the vernacular – do we know the native language of Fu-nan; and we are therefore unable to characterise the population from this point of view. I should be inclined to think that they were at least predominantly Indonesians, or rather – since this term does not mean very much – a people closely related to the Chams (or to the people who were in process of becoming Chams) rather than to the Khmers (that is, the people who were to establish Tchen-la). At this point it is easier to understand the reason for note 8 above.

[11] For the early periods I give the extreme dates at which a particular ruler is attested; later (mainly from chapter II onwards) the dates of his reign.

[12] Here again we have only the name used by the Chinese historians. Later, taking up an Indian literary theme, the Khmers claimed descent from the mythical hero Kambu and named their country Kambuja, which the Portuguese and Spaniards turned into Camboxa and Camboja; hence our Cambodia. Khmer is the name they apply to themselves and to their language. For my part I prefer to use the terms Khmer and Cambodian for the ancient and modern periods respectively, in much the same relative way as we use the terms Roman and Italian.

[13] This name, which has been taken over into the European languages as it stands, was given to their country by the inhabitants themselves, who had taken it from India (where it is the name of a flower, and also of many towns).

[14] This seems to find confirmation in a recent work: G. Coedès, "A Possible Interpretation of the Inscription at Kedukan Bukit, Palembang", in *Malayan... Studies... presented to Sir Richard Winstedt*, Oxford University Press, 1964.

[15] I should be inclined to date the two large bronzes in the Bangkok Museum – one of which is reproduced in this book – to the early years of the 8th century. But some scholars of great authority are doubtful of this and would apparently prefer the 9th century – or perhaps even the 10th, which seems to me out of the question. Cf. J. van Lohuizen de Leeuw, *Schätze aus Thailand*, Wallraf-Richartz Museum, Cologne, 1963, pp. 27-28, 87.

[16] The present tower is a reconstruction dating from the third quarter of the 12th century.

[17] These two temples, though belonging to the Angkor Vat style, represent its final stage, and their attribution to the reign of Suryavarman II is not certain: I am myself inclined to believe that Beng Mealea is later than his reign.

[18] Thai is the name they give themselves, with the meaning of "free man" as opposed to a serf or slave. Syam is the oldest name applied to them in Cham inscriptions of the 11th century and Khmer inscriptions of the 12th.

[19] See a recent study of these problems: J. Boisselier, *La Statuaire du Champa*, E.F.E.O., Paris, 1963.

[20] This is an interesting question which has not been thoroughly examined. It seems reasonable to suppose that in the old indianised states Buddhism spread among the people out of opposition to the ruling classes – the king and the brahmins – and was adopted by conquerors like the

Thai precisely because they were seeking to wrest power from the old dominant classes. We must not forget, however, that in the countries to which the Thai came, Burma and the Mon territory, Buddhism was already established and dominant.

[21] Their own name for themselves is Mran-ma (Bram-ma). The first visitors from the West made this Berma, Brama, which gave our Burma.

[22] The study of this field has still barely begun. See J. A. Stewart, "Kyaukse Irrigation, A Sidelight on Burmese History", *Journal of the Burma Research Society*, XII, Rangoon, 1921.

[23] There are excellent illustrations of Burmese art in L. Frédéric, *The Temples and Sculptures of South-East Asia*, Thames and Hudson, London, 1965; but the text must be used with caution.

[24] This at any rate is my own view. Alexander Griswold puts forward the interesting explanation that these types developed from a *stupa* surrounded with awnings for a ceremony. I do not find it convincing. He does, however, give a good account of the symbolic value of the Buddhist sanctuary. See A. B. Griswold, Chewon Kim and P. H. Pott, *Burma, Korea, Tibet*, "Art of the World", Methuen, London, 1964.

[25] To him, or rather to his family soon after his death about 1057.

[26] But their social structure remained very similar to the systems of ancient China, as has been well shown by Henry Maspéro in *Les religions chinoises*, in *Recueil d'œuvres posthumes*, I, Paris, 1950.

[27] It is still frequently stated that Nan-chao was a Thai kingdom, and as such it forms the first chapter of Thai national histories. But it has long been established by many Chinese, American and Japanese studies that it was essentially a confederation of tribes speaking Tibeto-Burmese languages – the Min-chia and the Lolo – in which a few Thai tribes played a minor part.

[28] On these developments, see my *Angkor et le Cambodge au XVIe siècle*, Presses Universitaires, Paris, 1958, chapter IV.

[29] Khmer bronzes in the style of Jayavarman VII have also been found in Ceylon, and there were frequent visits to Ceylon by Khmer and later Thai pilgrims.

[30] The history of Thai sculpture is still in its infancy. See, for example, A. B. Griswold, "The Buddhas of Sukhodaya", *Archives of the Chinese Society of America*. VII, 1953, and, on the other hand, R. S. Le May, "The Chronology of Northern Siamese Buddha Images", in *Oriental Art*, I, Oxford, 1949. For a brief survey of Thai art, see G. Coedès and J. Boisselier, *Arts de Thailande*, Musée Cernuschi, Paris, 1963.

[31] These chambers also yielded a rich store of gold jewellery which is a revelation. This is now very well displayed in the new museum at Ayuthya: see *Ayudhya Art*, Bangkok, 1956.

[32] C. Nelson Spinks, *The Ceramics of Sawank'alok*, Siam Society, Bangkok, 1965.

[33] This date, which I suggested for these sculptures, has since been confirmed by epigraphy: G. Coedès, "La date d'exécution de deux bas-reliefs tardifs d'Angkor Vat", *Journal Asiatique*, CCL, 2, Paris, 1950.

[34] Recent excavations at the Sras Srang at Angkor have revealed several Buddhist bronzes which give us a glimpse of this late development of Khmer art. This may throw fresh light on its influence on Siamese art of the 15th and 16th centuries, to which I think insufficient attention has been paid (Plates 139, 140, 145).

[35] It has not been possible to illustrate these in this book, since there are no recent photographs. There are excellent drawings in L. Bezacier, *Relevé des Monuments du Nord Viet-Nam*, E.F.E.O., Paris, 1959.

[36] Except, of course, in the technical field; for European inventions were quickly adopted, and also, as we shall note briefly, some of their decorative arts.

[37] The elucidation of Ptolemy's references has given rise to much discussion, which does not concern us here, nor alter the fact that mediaeval Europe knew nothing of South-East Asia.

[38] In this and later chapters, in order to facilitate comparisons, we shall give the dates of first publication (when applicable – otherwise of the journey or investigations concerned); that is, the time at which the discoveries became available to the general public.

[39] See B. P. Groslier, *Angkor et le Cambodge au XVIe siècle*, Presses Universitaires, Paris, 1958.

[40] Ralph Fitch's account can be found in Hakluyt; most conveniently in the Everyman's Library edition, 1962, vol. III, p. 305.

[41] Bouvet, *Voiage de Siam*, published by J. C. Gatty, Brill, Leyden, 1963, p. 109.

[42] P. Huard and M. Wong, "Les Enquêtes scientifiques françaises et l'exploration du monde exotique aux XVII et XVIIIe siècle", *B.E.F.E.O.*, LII, 1, 1964.

[43] E. Wurtzburg, *Raffles of the Eastern Isles*, London, 1954, p. 634.

[44] Malte-Brun seems to have taken the idea from the Scottish orientalist John Leyden. The term Indochina was not, however, immediately accepted. In Britain the area was long known as Further India; the German term is Hinterindien. The name South-East Asia became popular during the second world war as the area of Lord Louis Mountbatten's command. Finally it should be noted that Indochina, which is a useful description, is too often confused with French Indochina – Annam, Tonkin, Cochinchina, Cambodia and Laos – which may be used either geographically or historically. We have mentioned the origins of some of these names: to complete the picture it should be added that Laos is the country of the Lao Thai, with the addition of the plural *s*, and that Malaya comes from the Malay term Malayu.

[45] Critical bibliographical references to the works cited are not given here; they may be found in H. Cordier, *Bibliotheca Indosinica*, E.F.E.O., Paris, 1912-1932, 4 volumes and index.

[46] H. Mouhot, *Voyage dans les Royaumes de Siam, de Cambodge, de Laos...*, Hachette, Paris, 1868, p. 187.

[47] John Thomson, *The Straits of Malacca, Indo-China and China; or ten years' travels, adventures and residence abroad*, London, 1875. My *Angkor et le Cambodge au XVIe siècle*, op. cit., contains a detailed account of what was known about Angkor from the 16th to the 19th century.

[48] A bibliography on Indochina since 1900 will be found in J. F. Embree and L. O. Dotson, *A Bibliography of the Peoples and Cultures of Mainland South-East Asia*, Yale University Press, 1950; and C. C. Hobbs, *South-East Asia*, Library of Congress, Washington, 1952. A more recent work is P. B. Lafont, *Bibliographie du Laos*, E.F.E.O., Paris, 1964.

[49] The Directorate's *Bulletin*, published since 1900, and its other publications are essential sources of information about Indochina.

[50] There is a good summary of work in this field in E. Saurin, "Études géologiques et préhistoriques; cinquante ans d'orientalisme français", *B.S.E.I.*, XXXV, 4, Saigon, 1951.

[51] O. Janse, *Archaeological Research in Indochina*, Cambridge, Mass., and Bruges, 1947-1958, 3 volumes.

[52] V. Goloubew, "L'Age du Bronze au Tonkin", *B.E.F.E.O.*, XXIX, Hanoi, 1929.

[53] *Prehistorica Asiae Orientalis*, I.D.E.O., Hanoi, 1932. More recently, the Far Eastern Prehistory Association has held regular conferences and publishes *Asian Perspectives*, edited by the devoted W. G. Solheim, which is indispensable in these fields.

[54] R. von Heine-Geldern, "Das Tocharerproblem und die pontische Wanderung", in *Saeculum*, II, Vienna, 1951, and *Globus*, Vienna, 1952.

[55] B. Karlgren, "The Date of the Early Dong-son Culture", *Bulletin of the Museum of Far Eastern Antiquities*, XIV, Stockholm, 1942.

[56] A first trial was made at Banteay Srei by H. Marchal.

[57] His tragic death precluded the publication of most of his discoveries, which have appeared only in summary form in the *B.E.F.E.O.* "Chronique". Full justice has not yet been done to the very remarkable work done by Georges Alexandre Trouvé; and he was also the first to demand that the necessary resources should be made available for Angkor.

[58] *Journal des Savants*, 1861, p. 458.

[59] I have already discussed these problems from another point of view in *Colloque sur les Recherches des Instituts Français des Sciences Humaines en Asie*, Fondation Singer-Polignac, Paris, 1960. My remarks at this symposium drew objections, which will be found in the same publication. I feel bound to say that I still maintain my views, and indeed, after closer examination of the data, I feel even more confident of their truth.

[60] M. W. F. Tweedie, "The Stone Age in Malaya", *Journal of the Royal Asiatic Society, Malayan Branch*, XXVI, Singapore, 1953.

[61] L. Malleret, "Ouvrages circulaires en terre de l'Indochine méridionale", *B.E.F.E.O.*, XLIX, 2, Paris, 1959.

[62] Those who know Pierre Boulle's novel and the film will recognise the River Kwai. See H. R. van Heekeren, "Thaï-Danish Prehistoric Expedition", *Jal. Siam Soc.*, LI, 1, 1961; P. Sørensen, "Ban Kao", *ibid.*, LII, 1, 1964.

[63] This site was discovered in 1953 during the reconstruction of the temple of P'imai by the Thai Architectural Survey under the direction of E.F.E.O.

[64] A. Christie, in *Historians of South-East Asia*, edited by D. G. E. Hall, Oxford University Press, 1961.

[65] O. Janse, *Dionysos au Viet-Nam*, Viking, Oslo, 1958, and "Viet-Nam, carrefour de peuples et de civilisations", in *France-Asie*, XVII, 165, Tokyo, 1961.

[66] Nor must we forget the benefit Indian studies may draw from the conclusions reached in Indochina. Paul Mus had an excellent phrase for it: "India seen from the East".

[67] Note 66 applies here too. Paul Demieville put it excellently: "Everywhere we find in Indochina material to explain the origins of China, if it is true that Chinese civilisation developed from a prehistoric or protohistoric complex which embraced the whole of southern Asia" ("Les Etudes chinoises classiques", in *B.S.E.I.*, XXXV, 4, 1951).

[68] G. Coedès has recently underlined this point: "Some Problems in the Ancient History of the Hinduized States of South-East Asia", *Journal of Southeast Asian History*, No. 2, Singapore, 1964.

[69] L. Malleret, *L'Archéologie du Delta du Mékong*, E.F.E.O., Paris, 1959-1963, 3 volumes.

[70] The credit for drawing attention to these works belongs to the late P.D.R. Williams-Hunt, "Irregular Earthworks in Eastern Siam", *Antiquity*, 24, 1950.

[71] Some of these observations were due to a pilot, M. Déricourt, whose enquiring mind led him to become a pioneer in this field, and who lost his life on duty. See his "Observations archéologiques aériennes", B.E.F.E.O., L, 2, Paris, 1962.

[72] U Aung Thaw, *Preliminary Report on the Excavations at Peikthanomyo*, Archaeological Survey of Burma, Rangoon, 1959.

[73] Along with my friend the late C. A. Gibson-Hill, I personally examined all the sherds from these excavations in the Raffles Museum at Singapore. I can, therefore, claim to speak from personal knowledge. The soundness of Quaritch Wales's conclusions has also been tested by A. Lamb: see, *inter alia*, his article "The Temple on the Sungei Batu Pahat", *Journal of the Federal Museums*, Kuala Lumpur, 1960. In putting forward plans for the reconstruction of this temple, at the request of the Malayan government, I recommended that it should be systematically excavated to save anything that might have escaped Quaritch Wales's investigations. The article by Lamb, who carried out the work with great competence, is instructive on this point.

[74] G. Coedès, *Les Etats hindouisés d'Indochine et d'Indonésie*, Paris, 1964; p. 125, with reference to H. Parmentier's *L'Art khmer primitif*, E.F.E.O., Paris, 1927. See also an interesting comment by the same author, explaining his methods, on discovering that each tower in the reconstructed Banteay Srei had three stories, not two as he had drawn them: "Chronique", *B.E.F.E.O.*, XXXIII, 1, 1933, p. 518.

[75] G. Coedès, *Angkor, An Introduction*, Oxford University Press, 1963, p. 57. Philippe Stern, in his recent important study on the style of the Bayon, avoided discussing the internal chronology of the buildings, knowing how unreliable earlier studies were. Paul Mus visited the site for the purpose of his fundamental investigations. See his recent study, "Le Sourire d'Angkor", in *Artibus Asiae*, XXIV, 3/4, Ascona, 1961.

[76] Since this work also requires resources, the classic excuse is the lack of finance. But if we take an actual example we find that, reckoned at constant prices or in terms of man-days, the scale of effort at Angkor showed a steady rise, except in the period from 1923 to 1931: between 1908 and 1922, and again between 1932 and 1944, it was constantly increasing, and in 1944 it was higher than it was in 1960.

[77] Work in Siam is referred to in note 32. Y. d'Argencé has published an excellent study on *Les Céramiques à base chocolatée du Musée de Hanoi*, E.F.E.O., Paris, 1958, which is fundamental for this group of Vietnamese pieces of the 14th-16th centuries. Chinese exported pottery has also, fortunately, been the subject of many studies. I refer to local pottery, which is found everywhere, and has been neglected for sixty years.

[78] Mademoiselle M. Giteau has undertaken this task for Cambodia. Meanwhile Alexander Griswold is pursuing his valuable investigations on Siam.

[79] This is a point which ought to have been made more frequently in this book. But having undertaken to write a volume on Indonesia in the same series I was anxious to avoid overlapping between the two. However immodestly, therefore, I must refer readers to this other work.

[80] "Chronique", *B.E.F.E.O.*, XXXIII, 1, Hanoi, 1933, p. 494.

[81] It can be seen, therefore, that the problem goes farther than "the opposition between the Indianist school and the sociological school" (whatever the latter term may mean), referred to by G. Coedès in "L'Avenir des études khmères", in the *Comptes rendus de l'Académie des Inscriptions et Belles-Lettres*, 1960, p. 367. Moreover he attributes to me views I have never held: see, for example, B. P. Groslier, "Our Knowledge of Khmer Civilisation", *Journal of the Siam Society*, XLVIII, 1, Bangkok, 1960.

[82] As a measure of the difficulty, we may note that there are in existence something like a thousand Khmer inscriptions, which could be brought together in ten quarto volumes of 300 pages each. Compare this with the 40,000 Greek and 40,000 Latin inscriptions known, in addition to the whole of Greek and Roman literature.

[83] The phrase, to be taken with a pinch of salt, is M. Bloch's: "Apologie pour l'Histoire", in *Cahiers des Annales*, Armand Colin, Paris, 1964 (5th edition), p. 11.

[84] H. I. Marrou, *De la Connaissance historique*, Paris, 1944 (4th edition), p. 118.

[85] C. Lévi-Strauss, *A World on the Wane*, London, 1961.

[86] See J. Filliozat, "L'Orientalisme et les sciences humaines", *B.S.E.I.*, XXXV, 4, Saigon, 1951.

[87] 1964 edition, 19th impression. This is, of course, said without any ill will towards this benefactor of crossword puzzle fans.

[88] This can be measured to some extent by the words taken into French or English from the Indochinese languages. Apart from proper names, and the names of plants, materials and animals which are taken over with the things themselves, the numbers of such borrowings seem to be small.

[89] P. Pelliot, *Mémoires de Tcheou Ta-kouan sur les Coutumes du Cambodge*, A. Maisonneuve, Paris, 1951.

[90] Mouhot, *op. cit.*, p. 187. This gave rise to the legend of a people who built Angkor and then disappeared, and thus had nothing in common with the present-day Cambodians. Stories of this kind are unfortunately found all too often in the writings of journalists – and not only journalists.

[91] Nor must we forget the distortions that sometimes arise from political passions.

[92] Wurtzburg, *op. cit.*, p. 634. |

[93] "Chronique", *B.E.F.E.O.*, I, 4, Hanoi, 1901, p. 384.

[94] "Chronique", *B.E.F.E.O.*, VIII, Hanoi, 1908. I cite these examples from Angkor only because they seem to me relevant. If in this book I have given undue prominence to work done on French Indochina – as I fear I have – this is not from partiality, but because I am more familiar with it, and because the sheer volume of work done in this field is greater. On the other hand I can claim that I have not been sparing of criticism.

SELECT BIBLIOGRAPHY

L. BEZACIER, *L'Art vietnamien*, Editions de l'Union française, Paris, 1955.

J. BOISSELIER, *La Statuaire khmère et son évolution*, E.F.E.O., Paris, 1955.
La Statuaire du Champa, E.F.E.O., Paris, 1963.

L. P. BRIGGS, "The Ancient Khmer Empire", *American Philosophical Society*, Philadelphia, 1951.

G. DE CORAL-RÉMUSAT, *L'Art khmer*, Editions d'Art et d'Histoire, Paris, 1940.

G. COEDÈS, *Les Etats hindouisés d'Indochine et d'Indonésie*, "Histoire du Monde" (ed. E. Cavaignac), De Boccard, Paris, 1964 (3rd edition).
The Making of South East Asia, Routledge and Kegan Paul, London, 1966.

E. H. G. DOBBY, *South-east Asia*, London University Press, 1964 (8th edition).

P. DUPONT, "La Statuaire pré-angkorienne", *Artibus Asiae*, Ascona, 1955.
L'Archéologie mône de Dvâravati, E.F.E.O., Paris, 1959.

C. DUROISELLE, "The Ananda Temple at Pagan", *Memoirs of the Archaeological Survey of India*, No. 56, Delhi, 1937.

A. B. GRISWOLD, "Dated Buddha Images of Northern Siam", *Artibus Asiae*, Ascona, 1957.

A. B. GRISWOLD, CHEWON KIM, and P. H. POTT, *Burma, Korea, Tibet*, "Art of the World", Methuen, London, 1964.

B. P. GROSLIER, *Angkor, Art and Civilization*, Thames and Hudson, London, 1966. (2nd edition).
Indochina, "Art of the World", Methuen, London, 1962.

D. G. E. HALL, *A History of South-East Asia*, Macmillan, London, 1964 (2nd edition).
Burma, Hutchinson, London, 1950.

G. E. HARVEY, *History of Burma*, Longmans, London, 1925.

P. HUARD and M. DURAND, *Connaissance du Vietnam*, E.F.E.O., Paris, 1954.

P. LE BOULANGER, *Histoire du Laos français*, Plon, Paris, 1931.

G. CONDOMINAS, *Ethnologie de l'Indochine*, *in*

A. LEROI-GOURHAN and J. POIRIER, *Ethnologie de l'Union française*, vol. II, Presses Universitaires, Paris, 1953.

R. S. LE MAY, *Buddhist Art in Siam*, Cambridge University Press, 1938.

LE THANH KHOI, *Le Viêt-nam, Histoire et Civilisation*, Editions de Minuit, Paris, 1955.

U LU PE WIN, *Pictorial Guide to Pagan*, Calcutta, 1955.

G. MASPÉRO, *Le Royaume du Champa*, Van Oest, Paris, 1928.
Un Empire colonial français: L'Indochine, Van Oest, Paris, 1929-30.

F. J. MOORHEAD, *A History of Malaya and her Neighbours*, vol. 1, Longmans, London, 1957.

H. PARMENTIER, *L'Art du Laos*, E.F.E.O., Paris, 1954.

K. A. NILAKANTA SASTRI, *South Indian Influences in the Far East*, Bombay, 1949.

D. SECKEL, *The Art of Buddhism*, "Art of the World", Methuen, London, 1964.

P. STERN, *L'Art du Champa et son évolution*, Douladoure, Toulouse, 1942.
L'Art du Bayon et les Monuments de Jayavarman VII, Presses Universitaires, Paris, 1965.

H. TINKER, *The Union of Burma*, London, 1957

M. W. F. TWEEDIE, *Prehistoric Malaya, A Cultural History*, Philosophical Library, New York, 1950.

W. A. R. WOOD, *A History of Siam*, Bangkok, 1933 (2nd edition).

LIST OF ILLUSTRATIONS

11　*Buddhist relief representing the First Sermon of the Buddha. Nak'on Pathom, Siam. Sandstone; height 0.60 m. Mon art of Dvaravati; 7th–8th century A.D. (phot. B. P. Groslier).*

12, 13, 14　*Krishna raising Mount Govardhana. Sri D'eb, Siam. NMB. Sandstone; height 0.56 m. 6th–7th century A.D. (phot. B. P. Groslier).*

15, 16　*Buddha from Binh-hoa, Cochinchina. NMV. Wood; height 1.35 m. Fu-nan style; 5th century A.D.? (phot. B. P. Groslier).*

17　*Buddha from Thap-muoi, Cochinchina. NMV. Wood; height 2.91 m. Fu-nan style; 5th–6th century A.D. (phot. B. P. Groslier).*

18　*Balarama. Phnom Da, Ta Keo. NMPP. Sandstone; height 1.76 m. Fu-nan style; beginning of 6th century A.D. (phot. Luc Ionesco. EFEO).*

19　*Buddha. Son-tho, Tra-vinh, Cochinchina. NMV. Sandstone; height 0.55 m. Fu-nan style; 6th–7th century A.D. (phot. B. P. Groslier).*

20　*Sambor Prei Kuk, Kompong Thom. Tower N 7. Brick and stucco. Sambor style; beginning of 7th century A.D. (phot. B. P. Groslier).*

21　*Shoulder strap and belt buckle. NMPP. Buckle: Kbal Romeas, Kampot; gold; weight 184 gr. Shoulder strap: Chrui Angkor Borei, Ta Keo; gold; weight 300 gr. (phot. B. P. Groslier).*

22　*Avalokitesvara. Vat Kompong Luong, Prei Krabas, Ta Keo. NMPP. Bronze; height 0.21 m. 7th century A.D. (phot. Luc Ionesco. EFEO).*

23　*Head. Angkor Borei, Ta Keo. NMPP. Stucco; height 0.25 m. 8th–9th century. (phot. Luc Ionesco. EFEO).*

24, 25　*Vishnu in the form of the Kalkyâvatara. Kuk Trap, Cambodia. NMPP. Sandstone; height 1.35 m. Middle of 6th century? (phot. Luc Ionesco. EFEO).*

26　*Buddha on throne. Muong Intra, Singburi, Thailand. NMB. Bronze; height 0.30 m. 7th–8th century. (phot. B. P. Groslier).*

27　*Surya. Thai-hiep-thanh, Tay-ninh, Cochinchina. NMV. Sandstone; height 0.51 m. 7th century. (phot. B. P. Groslier).*

28　*Lokesvara. Ch'aiya, Surathani, Thailand. NMB. Bronze; height 0.63 m. End of 8th century to beginning of 9th? (phot. B. P. Groslier).*

29　*Prasat Thmar Dap, Kulen, Angkor. Brick tower. Kulen style; beginning of 9th century. (phot. B. P. Groslier).*

30 *Lokesvara. Bidor, Perak, Malaya. Taiping Museum. Bronze; height 0.80 m. 9th century. (phot. B. P. Groslier).*

31 *Vishnu. Prasat Damrei Krap, North. Kulen, Angkor. NMPP. Sandstone; height 1.80 m. Kulen style; beginning of 9th century. (phot. Luc Ionesco. EFEO).*

32 *Prang, Koh Ker, Kompong Thom. Sandstone; height 36 m. Temple-mountain of Jayavarman IV; between 921 and 944. (phot. B. P. Groslier).*

33 *Preah Ko: detail of eastern central tower with foundation inscription. (phot. B. P. Groslier).*

34 *Preah Ko, Roluos, Angkor. Main front. Brick and stucco. Preah Ko style; 879. (phot. B. P. Groslier).*

35 *Bakong, Roluos, Angkor. Temple-mountain of Indravarman, 881. Preah Ko style. Sandstone; height to top of central tower 34 m. (phot. B. P. Groslier).*

36 *Bakheng, Angkor. Sandstone; 76×76 m. at base, preserved to height of 13 m. Bakheng style; about 900. (phot. B. P. Groslier).*

37 *P'imai, Nak'on Rajsimha, Thailand. Central sanctuary. Sandstone; height 18 m. End of Baphuon style; about 1074–1100. (phot. B. P. Groslier)*

38 *Banteay Samre, Angkor. Main front. Sandstone and laterite. End of Angkor Vat style; middle of 12th century. (phot. B. P. Groslier).*

39 *Banteay Chmar, Battambang. Gallery of bas-reliefs, west side, northern half. Lokesvara. Sandstone; height 2.40 m. Bayon style; end of 12th–13th century. (phot. B. P. Groslier).*

40 *Lotus; purpose unknown; Angkor. NMPP. Bronze; height 0.32 m. 12th century. (phot. B. P. Groslier).*

41 *Mi-son A1: principal tower. Brick and stucco. Style of Mi-son A1; second quarter of 10th century. (phot. B. P. Groslier).*

42 *Tower of Bang-an, Quang-nam. Brick. Transition between Mi-son A 1 and Binh-dinh styles; end of 11th century. (phot. B. P. Groslier).*

43 *Baksei Chamkrong, Angkor. Brick and stucco; total height 24 m. Beginning of style of Rajendravarman; about 947. (phot. B. P. Groslier).*

44 *Prasat Kravan, Angkor. Relief on principal tower: Vishnu emerging from the cosmic waters. Brick; height 2.80 m. End of Bakheng style; 921. (phot. B. P. Groslier).*

45 *Pre Rup: detail of sculptured brick decoration on the principal tower-sanctuary; the stucco facing has disappeared. (phot. B. P. Groslier).*

46 *Banteay Srei: detail of architectural decoration of Library I (North). (phot. B. P. Groslier).*

47 *Banteay Srei, Angkor. Library I (North), east pediment. Murder of Kamsha. Pink sandstone; Banteay Srei style; 968. (phot. B. P. Groslier).*

48 *The same. Detail.*

49 *Trimurti: Brahma and Vishnu emerging from Siva's body. Prei Chruk. RAC. Sandstone; height 0.84 m. 10th century. (phot. Luc Ionesco, EFEO).*

50 *Head of Siva. Por Loboek, Siemreap. RAC. Bronze, gilded; height 0.32 m. Baphuon style, middle of 11th century. (phot. B. P. Groslier).*

51 *Ta Keo, Angkor. East front. Sandstone and laterite; total height 38 m. 100 × 100 m. at base. Khleang style; about 1000. (phot. B. P. Groslier).*

52 *Angkor Vat, Angkor. View from the air, looking east. Sandstone; 187 × 215 m. at the base; total height 63 m. Angkor Vat style; beginning of 12th century. (phot. B. P. Groslier).*

53 *Bayon, Angkor. North front. Sandstone; 140 × 160 m. at the base; total height 43 m. Bayon style; beginning of 13th century. (phot. B. P. Groslier).*

54 *Preah Vihear, Kompong Thom. Gate in wall surrounding principal sanctuary. Sandstone; Khleang style; beginning of 11th century. (phot. B. P. Groslier).*

55, 56, 57 *Angkor Vat. Gallery of bas-reliefs, south side, eastern half. The torments of hell. Sandstone; height of panel 0.90 m. (phot. Luc Ionesco. EFEO).*

58 *Bayon. Gallery of bas-reliefs; decoration of pillars of east porch. Sandstone. (phot. B. P. Groslier).*

59 *Angkor Vat. Gallery of bas-reliefs, north-west pavilion. Marriage of Rama. Sandstone; height of panel 0.70 m. (phot. Luc Ionesco. EFEO).*

60 *Buddha. Tep Pranam, Angkor. Sandstone; height 7 m. 13th century. (phot. B. P. Groslier).*

61, 62 *Details from pedestal, Mi-son E 1. Quang-nam. TM. Sandstone; average height 0.60 m. Cham art; style of Mi-son E 1; end of 7th century. (phot. B. P. Groslier).*

63 *Pedestal, Tra-kieu. TM. Sandstone; height 0.63 m. Style of Mi-son A 1; end of 10th century. (phot. B. P. Groslier).*

64 *Dong-duong, Quang-nam. Central tower. Brick; height 14 m. Dong-duong style; third quarter of 9th century. (phot. B. P. Groslier).*

65 *Dong-duong: reredos, Group III. Siva. TM. Sandstone; height 0.40 m. (phot. B. P. Groslier).*

66 *Pediment, Phong-le. TM. Sandstone. Style of Mi-son A 1; middle of 10th century. (phot. B. P. Groslier).*

67 *Mi-son A13: unfinished tympanum. Sandstone; width 2.40 m. (phot. B. P. Groslier).*

68 *Mi-son, tower D: pedestal. Sandstone; height 0.75 m. Style of Mi-son A 1. (phot. B. P. Groslier).*

69, 70 *Divinity, Huong-que. NMV. Sandstone; height 0.45 m. Style of Mi-son A 1; beginning of 10th century. (phot. B. P. Groslier).*

71 *Lokesvara. Excavations of Sras Srang, Angkor. RAC. Bronze; height 0.08 m. The first Cham object found at Angkor; probably end of 12th century. (phot. B. P. Groslier).*

72 *Pagan, Temple of Petleik E. Relief (terracotta). Candakinnara jataka. (phot. Lavaud. Musée Guimet, Paris).*

73 *Relief representing a* jataka. *Ananda temple, Pagan. Painted terracotta; 0.35 × 0.60 m. Erected by Kyanzittha; about 1105. (phot. Lavaud. Musée Guimet, Paris).*

74 *Ananda temple, Pagan.* Jataka. *Painted terracotta. (phot. Lavaud. Musée Guimet, Paris).*

75 *Stupa of Shwesando, Pagan. Brick and stucco; erected by king Anoratha in 1057. (phot. Lavaud. Musée Guimet, Paris).*

76 *Temple of Thetkyamuni. (phot. Lavaud. Musée Guimet, Paris).*

77 *Interior of temple of Nan Paya, Pagan. Brick faced with stone; built by Mon king Manuha; about 1057. (phot. Lavaud. Musée Guimet, Paris).*

78 *Decorative fresco from Dhammayangyi, Pagan. Decoration is late; 17th–18th century. (phot. Lavaud. Musée Guimet, Paris).*

79 *The Parinirvana of the Buddha. Ananda temple, Pagan. Stone. (phot. Lavaud. Musée Guimet, Paris).*

80 *Library of the Pithakathaik, Pagan. Brick and stucco. Erected by king Anoratha to house the sacred texts; 1058. Restored in 18th century. (phot. Lavaud. Musée Guimet, Paris).*

81 *General view of Thatbyinnyu, Pagan. Brick and stucco. Erected by Alaungsithu in 1144. (phot. Lavaud. Musée Guimet, Paris).*

82 *Decorative fresco from Dhammayangyi; Pagan. Decoration is late; 17th–18th century. (Phot. Lavaud. Musée Guimet, Paris).*

83 *Vase, provenance unknown. NMPP. Sandstone, glazed; height 0.35 m. 10th–11th century. (phot. B. P. Groslier).*

84 *Temple of Kubyaukgyi, Pagan. Brick and stucco. Erected by Kyanzittha's son Rajakumar in 1113. (phot. Lavaud. Musée Guimet, Paris).*

85 *Stupa of Seinnyet Nyima, Pagan. Brick and stucco. Erected by Anoratha; end of 11th century. (phot. Lavaud. Musée Guimet, Paris).*

86 *Vase, Thanh-hoa. HM. Sandstone, glazed; height 0.18 m. 10th–11th century. (phot. EFEO).*

87 *Pedestal urn, Thanh-hoa. HM. Sandstone, glazed; height 0.23 m. Thanh-hoa pottery; 10th–11th century (phot. EFEO).*

88 *Urn, Quang-huong, Thanh-hoa. HM. Sandstone, glazed; height 0.12 m. 10th–11th century. (phot. EFEO).*

89 *Temple of Htilominlo, Pagan. Brick and stucco. Erected by King Htilominlo in 1218. (phot. Lavaud. Musée Guimet, Paris).*

90 *Temple of Sulamani, Minnanthu, Pagan. Brick and stucco. Erected by King Narapatisithu in 1183. (phot. Lavaud. Musée Guimet, Paris).*

91 *Same as 89.*

92 *Fresco, Ananda temple, Pagan. 17th–18th century. (phot. Lavaud. Musée Guimet, Paris).*

93   *Decorative fresco, Nandamanya temple, Minnanthu, Pagan. 1248.*
      (phot. Lavaud. Musée Guimet, Paris).

94   *Mangalacetiya, Pagan. Brick and stucco. 1274. (phot. Lavaud. Musée*
      Guimet, Paris).

95   *Wat Mahathat, Sawank'alok: general view. 13th century.*
      (phot. B. P. Groslier).

96   *Wat Charn Long, Sawank'alok: stucco head. 13th century.*
      (phot. B. P. Groslier).

97   *Wat Sisawai, Sukhot'ai: stupa. Brick and stucco. 13th century.*
      (phot. B. P. Groslier).

98   *Lop'buri, Siam. Wat Mahathat, central sanctuary group. 13th century.*
      (phot. B. P. Groslier).

99   *Wat Mahathat, Sukhot'ai: detail of stucco decoration on brick.*
      (phot. B. P. Groslier).

100   *Wat Si Ch'um, Sukhot'ai: general view from overhead. 13th century.*
      (phot. B. P. Groslier).

101   *Wat Mahathat, Sukhot'ai: main front. 13th century. (phot. B. P. Groslier)*

102   *Wat Sri Sanp'et, P'itsanulok: general view. 13th century, with later*
      restoration. (phot. B. P. Groslier).

103   *Wat Sri Sanp'et, Ayuthya. Brick and stucco. 15th–16th century.*
      (phot. B. P. Groslier).

104   *Nak'on Pathom: large stupa, stucco decoration of base. 18th–19th*
      century. (phot. B. P. Groslier).

105   *That Luang, Vientiane, Laos. Brick and stucco, gilded. Founded in*
      16th century, restored in 18th–19th. Height of spire 35 m.
      (phot. B. P. Groslier).

106   *Nak'on Pathom: large stupa, rebuilt in 19th century on remains of*
      Mon stupa of Dvaravati. Brick and glazed tile. (phot. B. P. Groslier).

107   *Imperial Palace, Hué: Ngo-mon Gateway. Built in reign of Gia-long. 1833.*
      (phot. B. P. Groslier).

108, 109, 110   *Paintings on lacquered screen. Collection of Prince Piya Rangsit,*
      Bangkok. Bangkok style; 19th century. Scenes of court life, from Thai
      tales. (phot. B. P. Groslier).

111　*Buddhist painting: Buddha descending from the sky of Tushita. Phnom Penh. NMPP. Painting on cloth; width 0.70 m. 19th century. (phot. Luc Ionesco. EFEO).*

112　*Tomb of the Emperor Minh-Mang, Hué. Dynastic temple, main front. 1840. (phot. B. P. Groslier).*

113　*Imperial Palace, Hué: gateway of dynastic temple. 19th century. (phot. B. P. Groslier).*

114　*Imperial Palace, Hué: Ngo-mon Gateway. Built in reign of Gia Long. 1833. (phot. B. P. Groslier).*

115　*Nak-on Pathom: large stupa, rebuilt in 19th century on remains of Mon stupa of Dvaravati. Brick and glazed tile. (phot. B.P. Groslier).*

116　*Sambor Prei Kuk, Kompong Thom, Cambodia. Beginning of 7th century. Central tower of south group before clearance, 1961–1963. (phot. B. P. Groslier).*

117　*The same. Central tower of south group after clearance, 1961–1963. (phot. B. P. Groslier).*

118　*Bayon, Angkor Thom, Angkor. The temple before clearance, about 1916. Photograph taken by brother of Méliès; by courtesy of M. Desprez-Curely.*

119　*"Face" tower of the Bayon, before and after chemical treatment. (phot. B. P. Groslier).*

120　*Prasat Kravan, Angkor; 921. The area round the temple before the excavations by E.F.E.O. (1963), which revealed the associated structures – entrance pavilion, brick paths, etc. (phot. B. P. Groslier).*

121　*Prasat Kravan, Angkor; 921. The temple before complete restoration by Angkor Conservancy. (phot. B. P. Groslier).*

122　*Prasat Kravan, Angkor; 921. The area round the temple after the excavations by E.F.E.O. (Cf. 120). (phot. B. P. Groslier).*

123　*Prasat Kravan, Angkor; 921. The temple after complete restoration by Angkor Conservancy. (Cf. 121). (phot. B. P. Groslier).*

124　*Angkor Thom, southern gate: the giants lining the roadway, after complete restoration by the Conservancy, 1960–1962. (phot. B. P. Groslier).*

125　*Angkor Vat, Angkor; between 1113 and 1150. Steps along edge of canals in front of main entrance, before complete restoration, 1961. (phot. B. P. Groslier).*

126 *The same, after complete restoration, 1961. (phot. Luc Ionesco. EFEO).*

127 *Angkor Vat, Angkor. Air view of approach road and main entrance pavilion, showing temple and the canals which served as reservoirs of water for irrigation. (phot. B. P. Groslier).*

128 *Angkor Vat, Angkor. Air view from overhead of central sanctuary, looking towards west front. The photograph gives a good view of the internal layout of the building. (phot. B. P. Groslier).*

129 *Banteay Chmar, Battambang. Style of Jayavarman VII, about 1200. Bas-relief, west gallery, north side: musicians. Sculptures like this show us a part of Khmer life about which we learn nothing from the texts. (phot. B. P. Groslier).*

130 *Bayon, Angkor: external gallery of bas reliefs, north side, western half. A circus in the courtyard of a palace: an unfinished relief showing the technique of the Khmer carvers. (phot. B. P. Groslier).*

131 *Buddha, Angkor Vat. RAC. Late Khmer Art, perhaps 16th–17th century. (phot. Luc Ionesco. EFEO).*

132, 133 *Two heads of Buddhas adorned, Angkor Vat. RAC. These two heads, which are very similar in spirit and in style, but at different stages of completion, show the sculptor's technique. 17th–18th century? (phot. Luc Ionesco. EFEO).*

134 *Buddha adorned, Angkor Vat. RAC. Late Khmer art; detail showing the technique of this style, and the high quality it achieved. 17th–18th century? (phot. Luc Ionesco. EFEO).*

135 *Khmer reservoir, Angkor area. Contained within an embankment; designed to store the water of the river, which flows only during the rainy saison. This method of collecting water is the basis of the whole Khmer water supply system. (phot. B. P. Groslier).*

136 *Banteay Sras, western area of Angkor: a typical Khmer city from the air. The enclosed area is square, surrounded by ditches and earthworks; in the centre the site of the temple; in the background the embanked roadway. (phot. B. P. Groslier).*

137 *Stratigraphic excavations at Thommanom, Angkor, 1964. This section through an old Khmer reservoir shows the laying down of alternate layers of mud and sand, marking each rainy season. It shows the extent*

of the silting up which finally led to the abandonment of the reservoir:
see the upper levels of deposition. The photograph illustrates the economic
decline of Angkor. (phot. B. P. Groslier).

138 *Vase for holding betel quid, in the form of an elephant; Cambodia.*
NMPP. Sandstone, glazed; height 0.17 m. The most splendid example
of Khmer pottery; Angkor Vat style; beginning of 12th century.
(phot. B. P. Groslier).

139 *Buddha sitting on* naga; *excavations of Sras Srang, Angkor. RAC.*
Bronze; height 0.35 m. An example, hitherto unpublished, of a new type
(perhaps of 13th–14th century) which suggests a possible Khmer model
for some Thai pieces. (phot. Luc Ionesco. EFEO).

140 *Buddha adorned; excavations of Sras Srang, Angkor. RAC. Bronze;*
0.35 m. A hitherto unpublished example (perhaps of the 16th century)
which throws some light on the chronology of this period, practically
unknown except for a few works in wood which are difficult to date.
(phot. Luc Ionesco. EFEO).

141 *Pavilion, probably designed to contain a Buddha; Prei Monti, Roluos,*
Angkor. RAC. Bronze, gilded; height 0.10 m. Bayon style, end of 12th
century. (phot. B. P. Groslier).

142 *Altar with the Buddha, Avalokitesvara and Prajnaparamita; Prei Monti,*
Roluos, Angkor. RAC. Bronze, gilded; height 0.55 m. Bayon style, end
of 12th century. Recently discovered; the most important example of
its kind. (phot. B. P. Groslier).

143 *Sras Srang: an example of a Khmer burial of the end of the 11th century.*
(phot. B. P. Groslier).

144 *Anthropomorphic vase used as cinerary urn; Sras Srang, Angkor. RAC.*
Sandstone, glazed; height 0.24 m. A very distinctive type which seems
to have developed in Cambodia and north-eastern Siam about the 14th
century. (phot. Luc Ionesco. EFEO).

145 *Buddha adorned, sitting on* naga; *excavations of Sras Srang, Angkor.*
RAC. Bronze; height 0.50 m. Angkor Vat style, beginning of 12th century.
(phot. B. P. Groslier).

INDEX

277

THE TEXT AND ILLUSTRATIONS
IN THIS VOLUME WERE PRINTED
ON THE PRESSES OF NAGEL
PUBLISHERS IN GENEVA.

FINISHED IN OCTOBER 1966.
BINDING BY NAGEL PUBLISHERS,
GENEVA.

PLATES ENGRAVED BY CLICHÉ-UNION,
PARIS

LEGAL DEPOSIT NO. 394

PRINTED IN SWITZERLAND

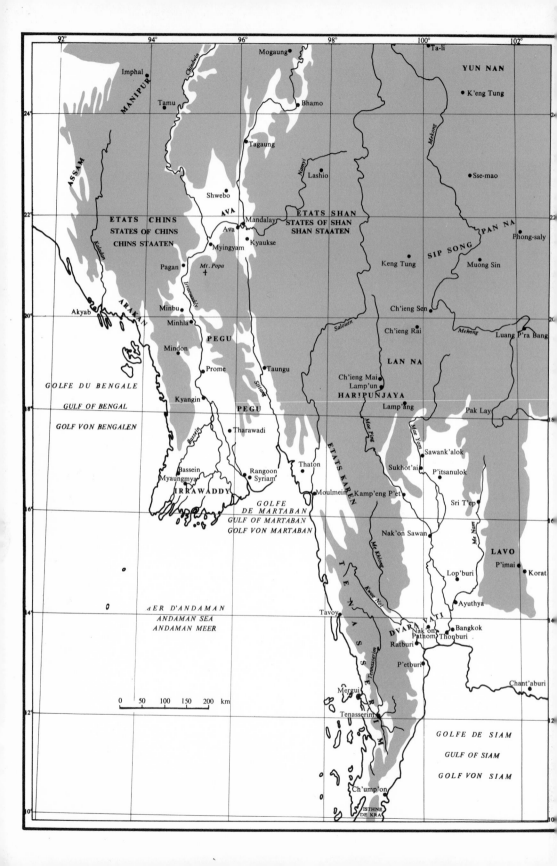